LET THE SHADO   JPEAK
DEVELOPING CHILDREN'S LANGUAGE
THROUGH SHADOW PUPPETRY

LET THE SHADOWS SPEAK
DEVELOPING CHILDREN'S LANGUAGE THROUGH SHADOW PUPPETRY

Franzeska G Ewart

Trentham Books

First published in 1998 by Trentham Books Limited

Trentham Books Limited
Westview House
734 London Road
Oakhill
Stoke on Trent
Staffordshire
England ST4 5NP

British Cataloguing in Publication Data
A catalogue record for this book is available from the British Library
ISBN 1 85856 099 3

Designed and typeset by Trentham Print Design Ltd., Chester and
printed in Great Britain by The Cromwell Press Ltd., Wiltshire

Contents

Illustration acknowledgements

Figure 1: Chinese shadow puppet from *Shadow Puppets* by Olive Blackham, Barrie and Rockliff, 1960

Figure 2: Indian shadow puppet from *Puppetry Today* by Helen Binyon, Studio Vista 1966

Figure 3: Indonesian shadow puppet (Bima) from Shadow Puppets by Olive Blackham, Barrie and Rockliff, 1960

Figure 4: Karagöz and Hacivat from *Let Karagöz LIVE!*, Kelvingrove Art Gallery and Museum © F.G. Ewart 1997

Figure 5: Grand vizier scolding workmen from *Let Karagöz LIVE!*, Kelvingrove Art Gallery and Museum © F.G. Ewart 1997

Figure 6: Workmen horrified at thought of losing heads from *Let Karagöz LIVE!*, Kelvingrove Art Gallery and Museum © F.G. Ewart 1997

Figure 7: Men missing Karagöz and Hacivat from *Let Karagöz LIVE!*, Kelvingrove Art Gallery and Museum © F.G. Ewart 1997

Figure 8: Karagöz and Hacivat as shadow puppets from *Let Karagöz LIVE!*, Kelvingrove Art Gallery and Museum © F.G. Ewart 1997

Figure 9: Javanese 'tree of life' and göstermelik from *Let Karagöz LIVE!*, Kelvingrove Art Gallery and Museum © F.G. Ewart 1997

Figure 10: Karagöz shadow puppet from *Let Karagöz LIVE!*, Kelvingrove Art Gallery and Museum © F.G. Ewart 1997, based on illustration in *Karagöz – Turkish Shadow Theatre*, Metin and DOST publications, 1975

Figure 11: Hacivat shadow puppet from *Let Karagöz LIVE!*, Kelvingrove Art Gallery and Museum © F.G. Ewart 1997, based on illustration in *Karagöz – Turkish Shadow Theatre*, Metin and DOST publications, 1975

Figure 12: Frenk shadow puppet from *Let Karagöz LIVE!*, Kelvingrove Art Gallery and Museum © F.G. Ewart 1997, based on illustration in *Karagöz – Turkish Shadow Theatre*, Metin and DOST publications, 1975

Figure 13: Himmet Aga shadow puppet from *Let Karagöz LIVE!*, Kelvingrove Art Gallery and Museum © F.G. Ewart 1997, based on illustration in *Karagöz – Turkish Shadow Theatre*, Metin and DOST publications, 1975

Figure 14: Beberuhi shadow puppet from *Let Karagöz LIVE!*, Kelvingrove Art Gallery and Museum © F.G. Ewart 1997, based on illustration in *Karagöz – Turkish Shadow Theatre*, Metin and DOST publications, 1975

Figure 15: Donkey that splits in two 'prop' from *Let Karagöz LIVE!*, Kelvingrove Art Gallery and Museum © F.G. Ewart 1997, based on illustration in *Karagöz – Turkish Shadow Theatre*, Metin and DOST publications, 1975

Figure 16: Göstermelik: fruit shop from *Let Karagöz LIVE!*, Kelvingrove Art Gallery and Museum © F.G. Ewart 1997, based on illustration in *Karagöz – Turkish Shadow Theatre*, Metin and DOST publications, 1975

Figure 17: Göstermelik: hat shop from *Let Karagöz LIVE!*, Kelvingrove Art Gallery and Museum © F.G. Ewart 1997, based on illustration in *Karagöz – Turkish Shadow Theatre*, Metin and DOST publications, 1975

Figure 18: Karagöz and Hacivat (traditional puppets) from *Let Karagöz LIVE!*, Kelvingrove Art Gallery and Museum © F.G. Ewart 1997

Figure 19: 'Galanty' figures from Shadow Theatres and Shadow Films by Lotte Reiniger, B.T. Batsford, London, 1970

Figure 45: Music *Our Father's Gifts*, arranged by Marilyn Smellie © Franzeska Ewart 1966

Dedication
To Mickey Aronoff, who also lets shadows speak

Acknowledgements
I would like to thank Katherine Awlson, Principal Teacher of English, Auchterarder High School; Mary Patience, OXFAM Scotland, and Caroline Pearson, University of Strathclyde, Jordanhill Campus, for their help in the preparation of the manuscript, and the staff and pupils of Glendale Primary School, Pollokshields, Glasgow for their help and contributions.

Grateful thanks also to my editor Gillian Klein for all her hard work and guidance.

Introduction

I was recently at an Expressive Arts forum where one of the workshops was called 'Drama for the Frightened Teacher'. It was well attended and much enjoyed. I would guess that for every Primary teacher who loves taking a class of twenty eight down to the gym hall for a spot of improvisation, there are nine who would rather face a firing squad – or, more realistically, an hour of creative writing.

As a Primary teacher in a multicultural school, I was one of those nine – yet I did enjoy Drama very much and was quite convinced of its usefulness. I also had in my classes several children whose first language was Panjabi or Urdu, some of whom had come to school without much English, and they needed all kinds of different activities to increase their confidence and aid their language development.

And so I began, very tentatively, to use shadow puppets. My first play was an adaptation of the story of Rama and Sita. It was to be my Primary Six class's contribution for a Divali assembly, and none of us really knew what we were doing. I would sit in front of the shadow screen – a piece of old sheet nailed to a picture frame – and shout instructions at the children behind it. I didn't dare to look at the chaos I knew must be reigning as the terrible ten-headed god Ravana careered across the performance area followed by a great army of demons, to snatch Sita away to Sri Lanka.

The puppets were made out of card cut from cornflake packets. The rods with which they were held against the screen were thick pieces of dowel that someone had found in the Technology corner. There were far too many characters on the screen at one time, and it all looked rather crude. Then Mansoor pressed the chariot that he had spent two afternoons making against the screen. He brought it slowly down to where Sita was standing, and I thought I had never seen anything quite so beautiful.

Since then I have used shadow theatre with every age group to express all kinds of different messages, and I would truthfully say I have never yet seen a performance that did not have something of that magical beauty in it. Shadow theatre can of course be very sophisticated but for me its real beauty lies in the fact that it enables someone with no confidence in art to succeed in creating something with visual impact, and allows someone with little confidence in language to express what is important to them.

Puppetry makes characters come alive. It is a very 'freeing' art, because you can hand over responsibility for what you say and how you say it to the character on your hand. Shadow puppetry is even more liberating. It really is 'Drama for the Frightened Teacher', as well as for the child who lacks the self-confidence to stand in front of a group of people and talk. Hidden from the audience, in the dark and behind a barrier, you speak indirectly to your listeners. Your words come not from your character but from the shadow of your character. You are well and truly safe; and it is often in that safe place that ideas and language flow.

In this book I hope to give the practical guidance needed for teachers to introduce shadow puppetry into their classrooms, and have the confidence to do so. But this is not just a 'how to make' book – I also want to share ideas about how shadow puppetry can be used to teach, develop and enrich language. And perhaps most importantly, I want to show how this particular branch of drama can be used in the classroom situation – a situation which my fifteen years of experience have shown me is not always conducive to the production of great dramatic pieces – such that each individual has an important part to play.

In an age increasingly dominated by computer technology, we should take care that other forms of communication have their rightful place in our class-rooms. Shadow theatre is as old a method of communication as we can imagine, born of the ancient need to tell a good story. We are as much in need of good stories now as we ever were. Now is as good a time as ever to 'let the shadows speak'.

1

As old as art itself

A story of how Art began appears in the writings of Pliny the Elder (*Natural History*, xxxv). There was once a young woman whose lover was going abroad. Before he left she drew his outline on the wall, using the shadow cast from a lamp. By 'capturing' the young man's shadow thus, she kept his image with her even when he was gone. And because the shadow was vertical, not horizontal as shadows often are, the link with death was broken – her lover lived forever.

Much has been thought and written about the shadow theatre, and always its qualities are seen as magical, lyrical, dreamlike. Rudolf Stössel (quoted in Reusch, 1991) said this:

> No other figure is so well-suited to convincingly portraying the magical as the shadow figure. For me the shadow play has always existed in the transition zone between this life and the next, between light and dark, life and death, waking and dreaming etc. One senses its transcendency.

To trace the origins of shadow puppetry one must go east. One theory about why shadow puppetry arose in China, Indonesia and India, and only travelled westwards much later is that the shadow is perceived in the West as something 'negative'. Phrases like 'a shadow of his former self', 'in the shadow of Death' and 'coming events cast their shadows before' show the shadow as something inferior, less important than the actual image, or as something sinister.

In Eastern thought this is not the case. The shadow is seen as intrinsically connected to the revered souls of the dead and particularly in the Hindu religion there is a sense of worship in the use of shadow puppets – a real 'link with the past'. The anthropologist Levi-Bruhl also linked the shadow with the soul when he observed how members of certain tribes were very careful not to step on their companions' shadows when they crossed a clearing in the jungle.

There are many conflicting theories about the historical origins of shadow puppetry, and these can be read in books listed in the bibliography. For the teacher of an upper Primary class it is surely more important to be able to impart something of the magic, the wonder, the 'other-worldliness' of the form than to get bogged down in hypothetical dates and places.

I think it is vital that children are shown the ancient forms and told about them before embarking on even the simplest shadow puppetry workshop. I have seen the eyes of Malaysian children, for example, light up at the sight of a *wayang kulit* (leather shadow puppet) – and when they see what great importance and reverence is given to this form, their motivation to create their own simple puppets and write their own stories about them soars.

To enable teachers to introduce shadow puppetry appropriately, I recommend the story-telling form – in other words, let the puppets speak for themselves. Here are three stories, versions of myths often told to explain the birth of shadow puppetry in China and Turkey, and of puppetry in India. After each story a brief description is given of the shadow figures and how they were used.

China

Over a hundred years before the birth of Christ there lived an Emperor called Wu-ti. Wu-ti had a concubine of whom he was very fond, and when one day the girl died, he was devastated.

He summoned his Court Magician and asked him if there was anything he could do to bring his beloved back, and the Court Magician went away and made a likeness of the girl in donkey leather which he had scraped and treated with tung oil till it was thin and translucent. He cut out her body in eleven separate pieces, painted her clothes and features with bright vegetable dyes, and attached the pieces to one another with knotted threads.

He placed an oil lamp behind the fine curtain of the Emperor's bed and when the Emperor was ready, he made the shadow image of the dead concubine appear before him by moving the rods he had attached to his puppet. When the shadow puppet danced across the screen its appearance and movements so resembled the girl that the Emperor really felt that she had returned from the dead to him, and he was greatly comforted.

It is generally accepted that shadow puppetry began in China, and it is known that in the 11th century it was used by storytellers to help to tell their tales – which were either about the wars between the various kingdoms, or came from Buddhist sources.

The puppets, which are quite small (about 30 cm high), were made of donkey skin or of leather from sheep, goat, pig, and even fish. They were delicately carved and their colours were very vibrant. Because they were used by itinerant storytellers who wanted to carry as little as possible, the heads were

Figure 1: Chinese shadow puppet

fitted with a collar which slotted into the body so that one body would do for several different characters. Shadow screens were made from mulberry paper, which often needed to be renewed. Nowadays it is very difficult to find leather puppets, and for the tourist market plastic is the preferred medium.

India

This story does not actually relate to shadow puppetry but it beautifully illustrates the idea of the puppet as a sacred object, a resting-place for the spirit. It also explains the role of the puppeteer and as such could be told both with the Indonesian *wayang kulit* and the Indian Shadow Theatre.

In Indonesian Shadow Theatre the puppeteer, called the *dalang*, has a priest-like role as he manipulates each puppet and gives it a voice. Both Indian and Indonesian shadow puppets are often used to perform epic stories like *Rama and Sita*, told especially at Divali time.

Lord Shiva and his goddess Parvati went one day to visit a toy maker. They were intrigued to see that the toy maker had started to make special little dolls with jointed arms and legs. Parvati in particular was delighted by these toys and she asked Shiva to allow their spiritual bodies to enter the dolls and make them dance. Shiva agreed and the dolls danced, but after a while Parvati was tired and so the gods withdrew their spirits and made to leave.

When the toy maker saw that Shiva and Parvati were going, he was sad. He could not bear it that the gods had given life to his dolls, and then taken it away from them again. He begged them to make the dolls live once more. The goddess Parvati then spoke to the toy maker. She told him gently that as it was he who had made the dolls, it was he who should give them life. Then both gods left. The toy maker thought about what Parvati had said, and he had an idea. He attached strings to the dolls, turning them into string puppets.

Then *he* made his dolls dance – *he* gave them life.

In India, rulers such as Vijaivada encouraged the use of shadow puppetry in the 16th century and usually plays took place outside the temple of Shiva, the patron saint of puppets. Indian shadow puppets are much larger than the other forms and when the operator holds them against the screen some of them tower above him. They are made of leather from goat, deer or calf, and in accordance with the Hindu religion the

Figure 2: Indian shadow puppet

4

Figure 3: wayang kulit – Bima

animals from which the leather is taken are supposed to have died from natural causes.

In Indonesia, on the island of Java for example, shadow shows lasting for many hours can still be seen. These *wayang kulit* performances are more ritualistic than the other forms and are seen as acts of worship. There is always a struggle between good and evil, the 'good' characters being ranged on the right of the dalang, the 'evil' ones on his left.

Indonesian shadow puppets are made from buffalo skin, and the rods used to operate them are buffalo horn which is curved to follow the contours of the body. They vary in height, usually being about 60 cm tall. Over twenty chisels are used in the tooling of the puppets – many different kinds of cuts are used to produce the delicate 'filigree' patterns which characterise the figures. Children are always fascinated to be told that when the face of a *wayang kulit* is being carved, the features are formed in a specified order. The nose is carved out first, followed by the mouth. Last of all the puppet is given its eye. Only then does its life begin.

In the Indonesian Shadow Theatre more than anywhere else, the puppet is treated as a sacred object. Feet must not be laid on heads when the puppets are packed away, and some groups of puppets must be stored separately.

In Indonesian Shadow Theatre there is an important figure called the *gunungan*, the Tree of Life, which is shown at the beginning of plays to bring the performance to life. It is also used as scenery throughout the play – a kind of 'multi-purpose' prop. It is thought probable that the *göstermelik* of the Turkish Shadow Theatre derives from this, and illustrations of each are shown in the next section. The idea of 'setting the scene' in this way is an interesting one for children to think about.

No *wayang kulit* performance would be complete without the *gamalan*, the orchestra of percussion instruments which interprets the dalang's words and carries the play forward. So important is the gamalan that *wayang kulit* performances are also enjoyed on the radio.

At the end of a *wayang kulit* performance a rod puppet often appears to point out the moral of the story. It may be interesting for children to consider whether there is something general to be learned from their own stories.

Turkey

There are many, many different versions of the story of how the Turkish Shadow Theatre began – all variations on the same theme – and this one is a combination of some I have read.

When our story takes place, round about 1330, Bursa was the capital of Turkey. It was a fine city famous for its wonderful mosques. Sultan Orhan was reigning, and he had ordered a beautiful mosque to be built. Many men were hired for this important task, and work was going ahead at a great rate. That is, until the workers' attention was taken up with something else ...

For very near the site of the sultan's new mosque was a row of shops, and in that row of shops Karagöz and Hacivat had their premises – right opposite one another.

And if there was one thing that Karagöz and Hacivat loved doing, it was talking! They could tell each other stories and insult each other all day long – and their stories and jokes and riddles were so funny that every passer-by just had to stop to listen to them.

That was all very well. People out doing their shopping have a right to

Figure 4

take a little rest and listen to a few stories. But, unfortunately for Karagöz and Hacivat, the passers-by were not the only people to stop and listen.

One by one the men who were building the mosque put down their tools and sat down and listened and laughed, and listened and laughed, and listened and laughed ... from early in the morning till late at night. And of course the result of that was that the sultan's mosque stopped being built.

Now, Sultan Orhan was in the habit of sending his grand vizier to inspect the work on the mosque. The grand vizier was a very important man and he was not at all pleased at the progress he saw. He

Figure 5

7

Figure 6

warned the men that they would have to work a lot quicker, and he said that he would expect to see a great improvement next time he came. Then off he went to report back to the sultan.

You would have thought that would have made the men pull their socks up, but it didn't. As soon as the grand vizier was out of the way, they downed tools and listened once more to Karagöz and Hacivat!

The next time the grand vizier came to the mosque not a tile more was in place, and he was furious. This time he threatened the men with the sack if they had not completed a good bit of the mosque when next he came. Even that did no good – it was far, far too tempting to sit in the sun listening to Karagöz and Hacivat.

On his third visit – when he noticed no difference at all in the mosque – the grand vizier lost his temper completely. He told the men that if there was not a vast improvement in their work by his next visit he would have them all executed!

The men were, understandably, quite horrified at the thought of losing their heads and looked at one another with very worried expressions. But did it make them decide to stop listening to the two shopkeepers, and work harder?

Not a bit of it!

Karagöz and Hacivat were so funny that, even under threat of death, the men listened to them – and of course when the grand vizier made his final visit not one stone had been set in place nor one timber sawed.

The grand vizier, of course, exploded. He ordered the men to be executed.

But the men were having none of it. They told the grand vizier that they were innocent, that it had not been their fault, and that they could not help it if there were two such hilarious men as Karagöz and Hacivat in the vicinity. They told the grand vizier that the real culprits who were holding up the work on Sultan Orhan's mosque were Karagöz and Hacivat, and that they should have their heads cut off.

And the grand vizier, believe it or not, took the side of the men – and poor Karagöz and Hacivat were executed instead. The grand vizier went to the sultan and told him that now his mosque would be finished soon, and the sultan was very pleased.

But as the months passed, Sultan Orhan began to feel very guilty about having had Karagöz and Hacivat executed – as well he might!

Not only that – everyone for miles around missed the jokes and stories. Bursa was a miserable place without the two shopkeepers.

Sultan Orhan had to do something. He sent for a member of his court called Seyh Kusteri and asked him to help. Seyh Kusteri knew exactly what to do. He took some camel skin and rubbed it well with a solution containing bran, to get rid of its oil. Then he dried it in the sun, and when it was quite dry he scraped it with a piece of glass until it was smooth, and so thin that the light could pass through it. The word for this is 'translucent'.

Figure 7

Then he painted pictures of Karagöz and Hacivat on to the leather with vegetable dyes. He painted them in a particular way, with their arms and legs separate from their bodies, and then he cut all the pieces out and put them back together using knots of gut.

Figure 8

Then he pushed rods into reinforced holes in the figures, held them against a screen of fine Egyptian cotton stretched tightly and lit from below by an olive oil lamp, and he made them move. And as he moved his Karagöz and Hacivat shadow puppets, he gave them voices and he acted out all the funny stories he could remember.

Seyh Kusteri acted out his shadow plays with Karagöz and Hacivat over and over again for Sultan Orhan, and the sultan was delighted. He felt that he had not really got rid of Karagöz and Hacivat after all.

Maybe he was right, or maybe it just made him feel better, but at any rate it is true that the humour of Karagöz and Hacivat will always live on in the Karagöz theatre. They can tell their old stories and riddles – and they can always invent new ones for new audiences – thanks to Seyh Kusteri, the patron saint of shadow players.

Of all the traditional shadow theatre styles, the Turkish shadow theatre is perhaps the best one to adapt to the present-day classroom. The figures themselves, particularly the old ones, are very attractive – but there is none of the exquisite tooling or the elegant shapes of the Chinese or Indonesian puppets. They are much more prosaic, so perhaps more accessible. And – most importantly – they have a very powerful voice when it comes to teaching about life in the Ottoman Empire.

It is a sad fact that the Turkish Shadow Theatre, and its Greek equivalent, are very much on the decline in their native lands, and that they are almost unknown here too. I have recently been trying to breathe new life into Karagöz and his friends, and I have found their characters and stories to be an excellent way of teaching all kinds of things, in particular about Islam. So most of the rest of this chapter is about the Turkish Shadow Theatre, or 'Karagöz' as it is often called, after its hero. It includes a play which I have written – *If You Want to Get Ahead, Get a Hat* – using the legend of Karagöz's origin, and also one of the bizarre original storylines.

The Turkish Shadow Theatre has been called the 'theatre of laughter'. Unfortunately, the humour is lost on the English-speaker because it relies so heavily on word play – so my 'Karagöz-style' play is liberally sprinkled with bad puns and 'knock-knock' jokes. It appeals to the humour of the average ten year old, and it allows children to write their own sketches in the same style. Another reason why Turkish Shadow Theatre lends itself so well to contemporary interpretation is that the characters are accessible and the humour adaptable. I have recently seen Karagöz and Hacivat dance to the music of the *Spice Girls* – a true meeting of cultures!

When the Turkish Shadow Theatre was at its height, in the 16th century, the country we now know as Turkey was part of the huge Ottoman Empire. In the Ottoman Empire Islam was all-powerful, and it is well known that orthodox Islam forbids the representation of living beings, and especially of human faces. Aisha, the wife of the Prophet, said once that Mohammed (pbuh) refused to enter her room on seeing a textile embroidered with images of living beings. He said that whoever made such images would be called to account on the Day of Resurrection of the Last Judgement. How then was Karagöz allowed in such a strictly Islamic climate?

We know that the Shadow Theatre was recognised by the religious authorities. It is often mentioned in *fetvas*, formal decisions on various points of the canonical law of Islam. Many Karagöz plays are described by Chelebi, a 17th century historian, in his *Book of Travels*. Not all are comic. Many, in fact, are products of Moslem mysticism, and some contain quotations from the Koran.

So the explanation is certainly not that the shadow theatre existed as some kind of 'underground' form. Many Karagöz puppeteers were in fact dervishes – extremely pious Moslems. During the fast of Ramadan, it is said the Karagöz puppeteers had to perform a different play every night, so their repertoires had to be wide and their memories good. The explanation for this acceptance of Karagöz by the Islamic authorities is thought to be that the shadow puppets were not seen as images of animate beings – because they were perforated with holes. So by making a Karagöz puppet the artist was not seeking to emulate Allah, because he was not making something lifelike. However, the words of the Prophet are still remembered. He said that an angel cannot enter a house containing images. So when weather permits, Karagöz is performed outside in the garden so as not to interfere with the angel's visit. And to keep the puppets in an inhabited house is considered impious.

Karagöz has many parallels with the *wayang kulit* of Indonesia and is assumed to have derived from it. Of particular interest is the parallel between the Javanese Tree of Life, which appears on the screen at the beginning of a performance, and the '*göstermelik*' of the Turkish shadow theatre – also a non-moving screen ornament which sets the scene.

On the pages that follow you will find two *göstermelik* and six characters. If you wish to make them into shadow figures to act out the play, you can photocopy them on to thin white card, possibly enlarging them. Then follow the directions for 'translucent shadow puppets' given in Chapter 6. To understand them better, here is a 'potted biography' of each of the human characters.

Karagöz – A practical, common-sense 'man of the people', who often appears less intelligent than he really is – for comic purposes. His name is

Figure 9: Tree of Life and göstermelik – lemon tree

Turkish for 'black eye', a sign of great beauty – and he regards himself as a most attractive man whose company no woman can resist. He wants to get on with life and make money for himself and his family, but is often unemployed and penniless. He is dynamic and energetic, not unlike our Mr Punch. He has a bald head and his hat is often hinged so that it can fall off to show it. One of his arms is usually very long – a characteristic he puts to great comic use. The puppet illustrated is perhaps the most 'typical' Karagöz, but he is seen in many other guises – as a jester, a turtle, a donkey – and as a woman. (This disguise gets him into all sorts of places he should not really be in!)

Hacivat – Karagöz's friend, but quite a different character. A 'show-off', always wanting to impress with his flowing language and knowledge. But his knowledge is superficial and he lacks common sense so Karagöz often gets the better of him. Not as energetic as Karagöz, Hacivat always thinks before he acts. He conforms to society's manners, is respected and asked for advice in, for example, money matters.

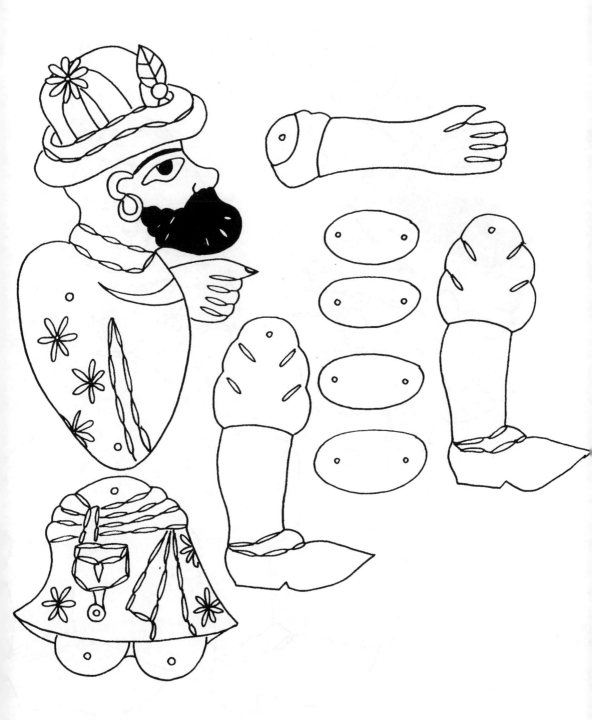

Figure 10: Karagöz

Figure 11: Hacivat

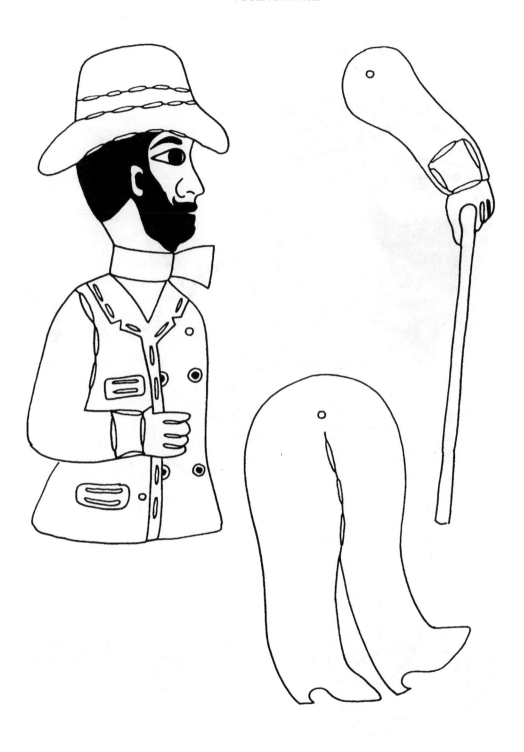

Figure 12: Frenk

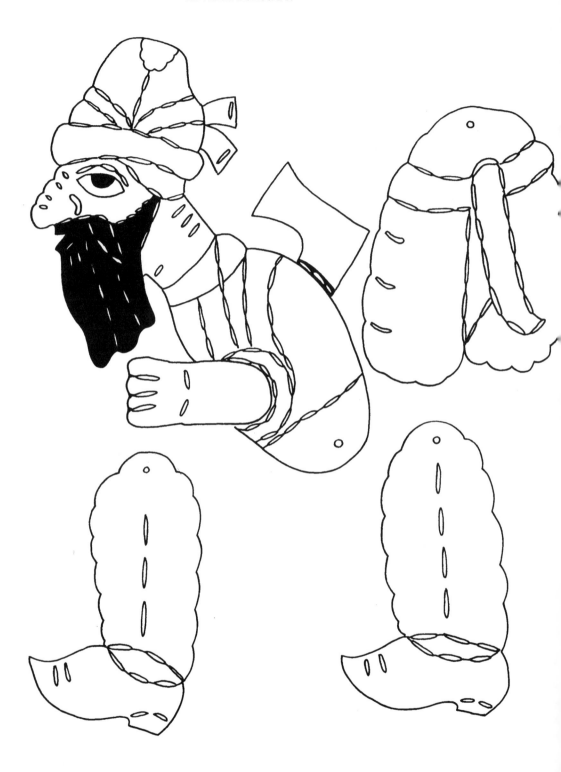

Figure 13: Himmet Aga

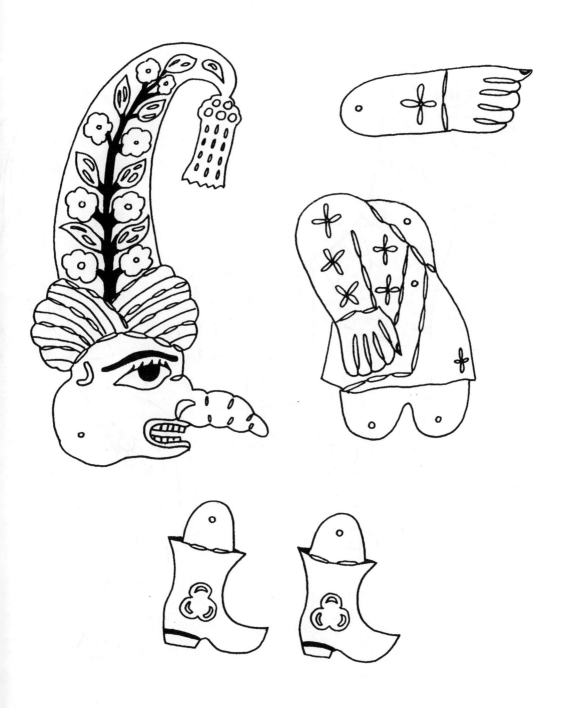

Figure 14: Beberuhi

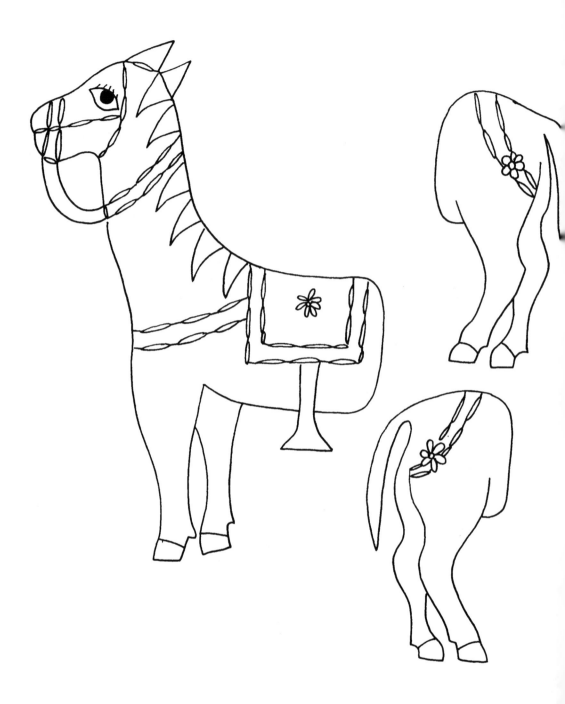

Figure 15: Donkey that splits in two

Figure 16: Göstermelik: fruit shop

Figure 17: Göstermelik: hat shop

Beberuhi – A very short man who is fidgety, talkative and extremely boastful. He has an annoying habit of asking the same questions over and over again. He does odd jobs around the neighbourhood. He is often the victim of Karagöz's punches when he annoys him.

Himmet Aga – The tallest of all the shadow figures, he is a very strong woodcutter from Anatolia. Sometimes Karagöz has to fetch a ladder in order to speak to him. He has a good heart and often talks about his sweetheart back in his own village.

Frenk – Often shown as a European, he can be a doctor but also a tailor, merchant, or tavern keeper. He is a coward and is not much liked.

Shadow puppetry was brought to England in the 18th century. There was a great fashion at the time for things Chinese and the silhouette figures were known as *ombres chinoises*, Chinese shadows. Apart from the fact that they were shown on a screen, however, they bore no resemblance at all to the Chinese shadow puppets. They were often quite complicated to operate, and the mechanisms for operating were kept well hidden – unlike the Eastern puppets where the shadows of the rods are not seen as detracting from the effect.

After a period of popularity the *ombres chinoises* died out by the end of the century. Shadow puppetry did enjoy a 'renaissance' in the 19th century at the time Punch and Judy shows were at the height of their popularity. When the day's performance came to an end as night fell, the Punch and Judy men would pull a curtain across the front of their booths, light a lamp behind, and put on 'Galanty shows'.

No history of shadow theatre would be complete without a mention of the work of Lotte Reiniger. Using beautifully intricate black cut-outs, she told fairy stories and folk tales, later using her 'trick table' with its glass top and fixed camera to make the first animated films. She did this by moving her shadow puppets, photographing each new position, and then playing them back as a film. Nowadays we are bombarded with animation techniques which are more and more sophisticated, but Lotte Reinger's cartoons are still admired for their beauty and subtlety of movement.

Today, particularly in France, Germany, Italy, Switzerland and the Czech Republic, wonderful examples of innovative shadow puppetry can be seen, and modern lighting technology often adds to artistic creativity to produce quite magical performances. All kinds of different materials are used, shadows of the actual actors are incorporated into plays, and so on.

IF YOU WANT TO GET AHEAD – GET A HAT

a shadow play in the **Karagöz** *style*

Cast

Karagöz – a fruit seller
Hacivat – Karagöz's friend, a hat-seller
Beberuhi – a (very small) builder
Himmet Aga – a (very tall) builder; originally a woodcutter
Frenk – the adviser to the sultan
A donkey (in two halves)

Scene I
Outside the shops of Karagöz and Hacivat

Two *göstermelik* showing a fruit shop and a hat shop appear on screen and remain there for some time while music plays. As the *göstermelik* are removed, the shrill noise of a whistle (*nareke*) is heard and Karagöz and Hacivat enter from opposite sides of the screen.

Hacivat	Good morning Karagöz, my fine fellow. How is life treating you?
Karagöz	Oh, not so bad, Hacivat – not so bad! Want to hear a riddle?
Hacivat	(*groaning*) Oh dear me – not another of your *dreadful* jokes, Karagöz! I really can't waste my time with them ...
Karagöz	Oh go on – it's a really good one!
Hacivat	(*reluctantly*) Oh very well, very well.
Karagöz	Magic! Here goes – Knock, knock ...
Hacivat	(*sighing again*) Who's there?
Karagöz	Banana.
Hacivat	Banana who?
Karagöz	Knock, knock ...
Hacivat	(*with another sigh*) Who's there?
Karagöz	Banana.
Hacivat	Banana who?
Karagöz	Knock, knock ...
Hacivat	Oh honestly – who's there?
Karagöz	Banana.
Hacivat	(*angrily*) Banana who?!!!
Karagöz	Knock, knock ...
Hacivat	(*shouting*) WHO'S THERE?

22

Karagöz	Orange.
Hacivat	(*surprised*) Orange who?
Karagöz	(*laughing*) Orange you glad it isn't another banana? Good eh?
Hacivat	(*sarcastically*) Oh yes, *hilarious* I'm sure ... now, if you will excuse me, I must go and see to my shop. I sell the finest hats in the whole of Turkey, I'm sure you'll agree Karagöz?
Karagöz	Oh, sure – and I sell the finest *oranges* in the whole of Turkey. Which is even better – after all, you can't *eat* a hat, can you?
Hacivat	No, but you can't *wear* an orange!
Karagöz	Not unless it's an *orange hat*! Boom! Boom!
Hacivat	True, Karagöz – very true. A finer pair of shopkeepers you won't find in the whole of Turkey, or I'll *eat my hat*!

They both laugh and move off. **Hacivat** *stops suddenly.*

Hacivat	Would you look at that, Karagöz!
Karagöz	What, Hacivat?
Hacivat	Those workmen at Sultan Orhan's mosque – Himmet Aga, the great tall woodcutter and his friend, little Beberuhi who never stops talking. There they are as usual, hanging over the wall listening to us ... they never do any work!
Karagöz	I know – it must be great! But I must go and set out my fruit so that it tempts the passers-by to buy! And, talking of 'buying' – goodbye for now, Hacivat!
Hacivat	Goodbye for now, Karagöz my friend! May all your 'buys' be *good* buys!

They both rush off.

Scene 2
Inside the mosque which is being built for Sultan Orhan. **Beberuhi** *and* **Himmet Aga** *are laying tiles on a pillar.*

Himmet Aga	I am *so* fed up laying tiles, Beberuhi! I should be out in the forest chopping down trees with my trusty axe – *that's* the kind of job *I* like. And near to my sweetheart, not far far away from her!
Beberuhi	I know, I know, Himmet Aga, but it's a great honour to be building a mosque for Sultan Orhan. It's going to be such a grand mosque when it's finished. But we'd better get a move on, hadn't we – remember old Frenk, Sultan Orhan's adviser, who came last week, remember what he said?
Himmet Aga	Oh yes, Beberuhi, he said if we hadn't finished this pillar when he came back he'd be really angry.

Beberuhi	I *think* he said he'd be *furious*, Himmet Aga. That's quite a lot worse than 'really angry', isn't it?
Himmet Aga	You're right, Beberuhi. He said 'furious'. So let's get on – hand me up another tile.

*We hear **Karagöz's** voice off stage.*

Karagöz	Oh listen, Hacivat – have I got a story for you!
Hacivat	*Another* story, Karagöz? I hope it's not a riddle!
Karagöz	No, it's a dead good story that will amaze and astound you, Hacivat!
Himmet Aga	Listen, Beberuhi – it's another of Karagöz's stories! Let's go and listen.
Beberuhi	But what about the tiles? What about Sultan Orhan's adviser?
Himmet Aga	Who cares? We'll do it later – come on, or we'll miss the beginning of the story!

They rush off, leaving their work.

Scene 3
*Outside the shops of **Karagöz** and **Hacivat***

Hacivat	Come on, Karagöz – tell me the story, for I must get back to my hats. I've sold three this morning, all to fine, educated men like myself!
Karagöz	Well, it goes like this ... one day I was leading my donkey along ...

*A donkey appears and **Karagöz** begins to lead it slowly.*

> ... on the way to Constantinople to visit my brother, and it was all going quite the thing when suddenly ...

The donkey splits into two pieces.

> ... my donkey split in two!

Hacivat	Oh dear – just *like* the thing! And what did you do, Karagöz?
Karagöz	Well, *obviously* – I took it to a donkey-repairer. But the donkey-repairer didn't know what he was doing!
Hacivat	Why? What did he do?

The donkey is fitted together again, but with its hind legs facing upwards.

Karagöz	He fitted the donkey's back legs on the *wrong way*, Hacivat! And we had to get home like that, with his back legs facing up to the sky!
Hacivat	(*laughing*) A fine story, Karagöz! A fine story. It reminds me of one I heard the other day – I'll tell you it later. Bye!
Karagöz	Bye for now!

They go back to their shops.

Scene 4
In the mosque

Beberuhi   (*laughing*) Do you think that was true? Oh anyway – it was a great story!

Himmet Aga   Sure was – but *all* Karagöz's stories are great. I could listen to them for hours!

Beberuhi   Eh ... Himmet Aga ... we *do* listen to them for hours. And look at the pillar – there are hardly any tiles on it. What will the sultan's adviser say?

Sound of a fanfare. They both jump.

Himmet Aga   Oh no! Oh no! Oh no! Beberuhi, we're done for – it must be Frenk, Sultan Orhan's adviser, come to check up on us!

Enter Frenk.

Frenk   Well, well, well – what do I see before me?

Beberuhi   A beautiful pillar covered in tiles, fit for Sultan Orhan sir?

Frenk man?   (*furiously*) What do you mean, you lazy, good-for-nothing little 'A beautiful pillar covered in tiles, fit for Sultan Orhan'?

Himmet Aga   (*whispers*) Nice try, Beberuhi, nice try.

Frenk   Not one single tile has been set in place since the last time I was here. This is disgraceful! That does it – you will both have your heads chopped off!

Himmet Aga and Beberuhi gasp.

    Yes, you shall be beheaded. You were well warned last time. Now, I am a very busy man, so please walk this way ...

Beberuhi   But wait, sir – please wait! It was not our faults.

Frenk   What do you mean? Of course it was your faults. Who else could possibly be to blame?

Beberuhi and Himmet Aga   *Karagöz and Hacivat!*

Frenk   Who?

Beberuhi and Himmet Aga   *Karagöz and Hacivat!*

Beberuhi   Yes, your honour – *they* kept us from our work with their stories.

Himmet Aga   That's right, your excellency. If anyone should be beheaded, it's Karagöz and Hacivat!

Frenk   *Really?* Karagöz and Hacivat? (*thoughtfully*) Yes, I have heard about them – everyone talks about their stories.

Beberuhi   Yes, your honour – they're real nuisances. No one can get on with their work any more – no one!

Himmet Aga	They ought to be stopped, your worship. They lower the tone of the neighbourhood.
Frenk	Mmm – I take your point, I take your point. I shall go and have them arrested straight away.
	(*starts to leave, then turns back*)
	And you two – get back to your work this instant!
Beberuhi and Himmet Aga	(*rushing off*) Yes sir, certainly sir, right away sir!

Scene 5
In the mosque some time later. Almost all the tiles are laid.

Beberuhi	Oh dear, Himmet Aga – how boring life is!
Himmet Aga	Yes, no more jokes. No more stories. How I miss Karagöz and Hacivat! How long has it been since Sultan Orhan had them beheaded?
Beberuhi	Nearly a year. And you know, they do say that Sultan Orhan is very sorry he did it now. Even *he* misses their wonderful tales.
Himmet Aga	Ah well, Beberuhi – there's one thing sure, no one will ever hear from Karagöz and Hacivat again. (*sighs*)
Beberuhi	Hang on – do you hear what I hear?

There is the sound of a far-off whistle.

Himmet Aga	What?
Beberuhi	Listen – I'm sure it's him ...

*We hear the voices of **Karagöz** and **Hacivat** off stage.*

Karagöz	(*blows whistle several times*) I say, I say, I say – do you know what happened to the chicken who laid an egg on the sultan's throne?
Hacivat	I don't know – what happened to the chicken who laid an egg on the sultan's throne?
Karagöz	He got EGGSecuted! Boom! Boom! (*blows whistle again*)
Beberuhi	It *is*! It's Karagöz and Hacivat – returned from the grave. Oh dear me – I hope they've got their heads screwed back on!
Himmet Aga	Come on – let's go and see!

They rush off.

Scene 6
*The market place – **Karagöz** and **Hacivat** are shadow puppets on a huge screen.*

Himmet Aga	(*entering*) It is them! Oh my goodness – it's magic!
Beberuhi	(*hiding behind Himmet Aga*) I don't like this at all. It's spooky!

Himmet Aga	Wait a minute, Beberuhi – don't panic. It isn't *really* Karagöz and Hacivat. Look, they're puppets! There's a light behind the screen.
Karagöz	Well spotted, Himmet Aga. Hacivat and I are indeed shadow puppets, thanks to you and your little friend!
Himmet Aga	(*embarrassed*) Oh, we are sorry, Karagöz.
Beberuhi	*Deeply* sorry ... most unfortunate mistake, wasn't it. Still, no good crying over spilt milk, eh?
Karagöz	It's all very well saying that when it's not *your* milk that's been spilt, if you know what I mean. But actually, Hacivat and I don't really mind, do we Hacivat?
Hacivat	No indeed, Beberuhi. There is much to be said for being made out of camel skin.
Karagöz	Yes, the sultan missed our stories so much, he asked Seyh Kusteri to bring us back to life. And he made a lovely job, didn't he?
Himmet Aga	Absolutely – it's an uncanny likeness. I'm so glad to see you back with us again – can't wait to hear some more stories!
Beberuhi	(*tugging at Himmet Aga*) Himmet Aga, I think we should go and lay some more tiles. We don't want any more ... eh, milk to be spilt – do we?
Karagöz	No indeed we don't – off you go. But come back after evening prayers tonight and enjoy the show.
Beberuhi	We will, and every night from now on ... see you! (*rush off*)
Karagöz	Well, Hacivat – I suppose we'd better practise. It looks as though we're going to be kept busy for the next few hundred years.
Hacivat	Yes, Karagöz, I think you're right. I tell you what, though – I am very glad we both got our heads back.
Karagöz	But of course we did, Hacivat – that was because of what *you* used to sell in your shop!
Hacivat	Whatever do you mean, Karagöz?
Karagöz	Haven't you ever heard, Hacivat – 'If you want to get ahead, *get a hat!*' Boom! Boom!
Hacivat	(*groaning*) I walked straight into *that* one!
Karagöz	Now that reminds me of a *great story*, Hacivat! Did I ever tell you about the time I went in my boat to fish in the river and suddenly there was a huge gust of wind and a terrible roaring sound and ...

The puppets' voices fade and soft music plays. Slowly, the puppets are pulled away from the screen so that their shadows become paler and paler.

Figure 18: Karagöz and Hacivat as shadow puppets

With a knowledge of the ancient behind us, and an eye on the possibilities the 21st century will offer in terms of computer-generated images and digital photography, let us now come down to earth and look at how we can create our own unique magic.

Figure 19: 'Galanty' figures

2

The Puppet Company

It is a Monday morning at the start of the spring term, and the beginning of a new topic, a topic which has to carry a class right through the long wintry months till Easter. The teacher comes in carrying an envelope, sits down and gathers the children around her, solemnly taking out an official-looking letter.

'Listen to this, boys and girls,' she says. 'It came this morning, addressed to all of you.' Everyone sits up importantly, and she begins to read. But each child can hear from the falling tone of her voice that all is not well...

'Dear Boys and Girls,' the letter says, 'We at *Priceless Puppets* are delighted to send you details of our new show, *The Little Mermaid*. It is a Shadow Puppet show with lots of wonderful special effects that we're sure you're going to love. You'll just adore Clive the Conger Eel; you'll howl with laughter at Jerry the Jellyfish; and your hearts will go out to Miranda the little mermaid as she is captured by the Evil King Shark and taken to his Coral Kingdom ...'

The teacher looks round at the assembled children, who are gazing at her expectantly. 'Are they going to come to the school?' asks one, and the teacher shakes her head sadly.

'I'm afraid not,' she says, with carefully-rehearsed sadness, and when the sighs of disappointment have faded she explains. 'Look at the price – £150 a show! We just can't afford that at the moment, with all the books we need to buy and the summer trips we've got to organise. No, I'm afraid we won't be having *Priceless Puppets* this term. It's such a pity though,' she goes on, looking carefully at a few selected pupils. 'It would have been *so nice* to have a puppet show – particularly for the little ones. And shadow puppets – they would have been great ...'

She pauses, and notices with satisfaction that a few hands are beginning to be raised. Eventually someone says the magic words, 'Miss – could *we* not put on a puppet show ourselves?'

The teacher smiles with relief and her nods give the other children confidence – the floodgates open and she is deluged with suggestions:

'We could make our very own Puppet Company ...'

'... and we could give it a name ...'

'... and we could write our own stories ...'

'... and turn them into plays ...'

'... and make our own puppets ...'

'... and we could advertise ...'

'... and we could even go on tour ...'

And so the new term's topic, the *Puppet Company*, is born, and suddenly the weeks ahead seem almost too short to accomplish everything the topic will demand.

The *Puppet Company* topic has been very popular in Scotland since it appeared in the BP Contexts Box, a set of Environmental Studies topics commissioned by the SCCC and funded by BP. The topics are graded according to age and are deliberately non-prescriptive, being essentially frameworks for contexts building. The *Puppet Company* is targeted at P4/5 – eight to ten year olds – but I consider it to be better suited to the senior classes. It was originally conceived as a topic with a 'Technology' bias – the BP outline includes a series of workcards showing methods for making joints, designing trolleys and so on, and advocates a 'problem-solving' approach. However, this topic gives so many opportunities to use language in so many different ways that it really can fulfil all the language requirements a class could have in a term.

To give an idea of how the topic could be organised, I propose to describe some of the activities I have found to be most successful. A fictional account of the topic, containing a fair amount of historical and cultural information in its storyline, is *Putli's Puppet Magic* (Word Play, 1996) which I wrote to provide teachers with a book to read along with the *Puppet Company* topic. In the book, Putli (whose name is Panjabi for 'puppet') is a magic glove puppet who can whisk children through space and time to teach them a little about the main puppetry traditions, from ancient China to 16th century Italy and the

Commedia dell'Arte. From each tradition, Putli brings something back to the classroom for the children to make or, if it is a play, to act out. I wanted him to do this is because I want children to get a sense of the importance of the traditions they are imitating. I am annoyed by people's attitudes to puppetry as merely 'child's play', as something with much action and laughter designed to keep young children noisily happy for an afternoon. And while there is nothing better than a good, participative, puppet show – and every effort should be made to find one for the children to see when they are doing the topic – to view all puppetry as no more than this is to limit it severely.

So it is good to collect a few Eastern puppets – usually Resource Centres will have sets of Rajasthani marionettes to lend out, and these can also still be bought very cheaply. Shadow figures are more of a problem, *wayang kulit* figures being quite pricey, but you can occasionally pick up a cheap 'touristy' one for a few pounds. If all else fails, at least provide plenty of pictorial resources – journals like *Child Education* and *Junior Education* feature puppetry from time to time and have beautiful photographs.

The first activity for the *Puppet Company* is to find a name and design a logo, a challenging activity. Logos have to do a great deal – they have to be simple so that they are easily reproduced, and yet they must somehow 'sum up' the image the company wants to project. My first Puppet Company was called *Putli Puppets* at the suggestion of one of the bilingual children, and Putli, the little puppet clown who was the logo, became a real character in the classroom, long after the topic was over.

Once the corporate identity is established, the task of allocating everyone a job begins and, as with everything else I describe, this can take as much or as little time as you want it to. If Spoken Language is a priority – for example in a younger class where there may be some children who still do not find it second nature to give their name and address and answer questions clearly – it can be a good exercise to devise advertisements and application forms for positions within the company. The whole language of advertising comes into the topic on a number of occasions, so it is worth collecting up a large number of good examples of the genre.

After filling in their forms, children can be called for interview. In this role-play situation they have to give their personal details clearly and also make out a case for *why* they think they would make a good secretary or accountant or publicity officer! The results can be quite amusing but also very 'educational'. The roles of 'puppeteers' are not allocated. Usually it becomes obvious as time goes on who is going to shine at the various performance skills and so it is best to choose only 'administrative' posts initially.

At the point when you are set to start the actual running of the company it is ideal to arrange a visit from a puppeteer, and if you cannot find anyone willing to give up a couple of hours to show the children their set-up, then at least try to go to a public puppet show. Most companies are so fascinated by the fact that you have set up your own company that there is usually no problem in arranging a backstage visit – and your 'secretary' can prepare the ground with an ultra-polite phone call.

Before a visit or a show, it is best to discuss what kind of information you are looking for – after all, you are not simply going along to the puppet theatre to be entertained! Points which I always try to bring out are the type of puppets and how they were made and used, the transportability of the equipment and the lighting methods.

Thus inspired, it is time to discuss the all-important matter of what kind of puppet show you are going to perform, and who your audience is going to be. I will keep returning to the importance of audience. I think children need a good deal of guidance in order to achieve audience awareness in all kinds of writing, and when your audience is going to be sitting in front of you it is vital to get it right. Obviously you may not choose to work in shadow, but for the purposes of this book I will assume that that has been decided upon – so you will need to think about your screen and your lighting before you go much further. It is best to know what size and shape your performance area is before you even start to discuss possible stories – the size of your puppets will largely dictate what you can effectively do.

In Chapter 3 I give instructions for a variety of different shadow screens, and you may choose to give the children these instructions and have them follow them. That is a very valid language activity, but if you want to make much more of the possibilities your *Puppet Company* topic provides, you will not adopt this approach but will allow the children to arrive at a suitable design themselves. One way to go about this is to begin by drawing up a list of specifications. You could start by discussing your requirements as a class then when you see the children have got the hang of it, split them up into smaller groups, perhaps with one person in overall charge. Specifications you would be looking for would be 'reasonable size'; 'clear, good lighting'; 'good visibility so your audience can all see'; 'stability'; 'affordable materials'; 'transportability'; 'ease of storage' and so on.

When you have drawn up the final specifications list and are reasonably sure everyone understands what each point means, it is time to draw plans. Children might work in pairs for this, giving each pair a copy of the specifications list. Depending on the age and ability of the class, you may decide to insist on scale drawing and annotated diagrams from different angles, or you may keep it to a simple sketch.

From the sketches the children can build fairly crude models using art straws and sugar paper. From these they will get some idea of whether their designs are practicable – the main sticking point with free-standing shadow screens is that they tip forward, and if that is the case there will need to be some kind of counter-balance mechanism.

When I ran my first puppet company, I had a boy in my class called Ranjit. He had come to school speaking very little English and although by Primary Five (age 9) he was reasonably fluent, he still lacked confidence in reading and spoken language and was regarded by the other children as a quiet, rather nondescript child. But when we reached this stage of the *Puppet Company* topic, Ranjit really began to come into his own. Using diagrams and models to solve practical problems, he soon showed that he was quite exceptionally gifted in Technology; he knew how to get things to work. And I will never forget his brilliant solution to our problem of counter-balance, which unfortunately wreaked havoc for the rest of the school! For some reason our shadow screen had been built without resolving the problem of toppling forward, and we were already preparing to pack up our show to perform in another school when we realised we were still not assured that our set-up was safe. It needed greater stability – and the class turned to Ranjit, who always had the answers. He rose to the occasion as usual.

'Weights,' he said. 'We need to hang weights to the back.' And off he went, returning some time later with two extremely heavy plastic bags which he tied to two corners of the screen. It worked a treat, and we set off. It was only when we returned to school later that day that I realised where Ranjit had got his extremely heavy plastic bags: all maths activity involving weighing had had to be abandoned that afternoon – *Putli Puppets* had every single weight on tour with them!

To avoid this kind of disaster, planning is crucial. Having discussed possible difficulties at the art-straw-and-paper stage, the children can go on to build more substantial models out of 1cm square sectioned ramin rods and card. A useful method to show them at this stage is Jinx corners.

For speed it is best to have a supply of little right-angled triangles ready cut, with sides about 2cm long, made of stiff paper or thin card, using PVA glue or a low-temperature glue gun. Arrange the triangles as shown in Fig. 20 to create remarkably strong structures. Double corners can secure three rods at a time. You can also apply a giant-sized variation on the Jinx method to

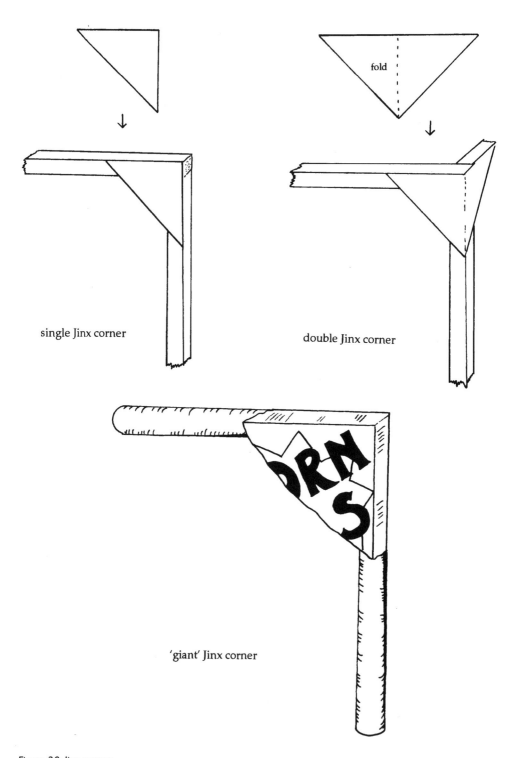

fold

single Jinx corner

double Jinx corner

'giant' Jinx corner

Figure 20: Jinx corners

Figure 21: screen advert

construct a shadow screen frame quickly. Use corners cut from cereal packets and fit into them the inside of kitchen rolls. You will have to join at least two together with strong tape in order to get a screen of workable size, then stick on a large sheet of tracing paper.

If there is one piece of equipment a puppet company can not be without it is a glue gun, and if you do not have one you should order at least three. Low-temperature guns are available through schools stockists and are perfectly safe for children to use – but you will need an 'adult' one for your own use too.

This kind of 'problem-solving activity' is excellent for developing the (positively) critical faculty in yourself and in the children. During the course of a *Puppet Company* topic I have seen children become increasingly self-critical as designs are put to the test and found wanting. There is, as always in teaching, a fine line between praising a child and letting it be known that it could be better, but when it is a practical exercise, and especially when the end result is something in which the whole class will have an investment, it is easier to make the point that 'it just won't work'. It really is a case of 'the proof of the pudding's in the eating'!

When the final models are completed the groups can deliver a 'presentation', telling the rest of the company why their design should be chosen to be built. A good way to prepare for this is for the children to write advertisements for their screens, perhaps giving them names and listing their 'selling points'.

The model which is judged to be best in terms of the original specifications will then be built. This may be the time for a parent to be drafted in, because a good deal of supervision will be needed if the children are to have a chance to be involved in the actual construction. It is also worth getting your 'secretary' to look through the Yellow Pages and contact local timber yards – for the promise of a mention on your programme, one might well give you a good deal.

You are now at the stage of deciding how to organise your puppet-making work and should start to think about possible plays. As far as the puppets are concerned, you will want to allow the class to try out several different types of puppet as well as shadow, and it is a good idea to get the children to write out a 'wish list' in the first week to deliver to their parents and throughout the school – for material scraps, tights and odd socks, buttons, ribbons and so on. The school should provide things like paper clips, polystyrene balls, glue, card, paper fasteners, garden rods etc. so that all kinds of ideas can be tried.

Since we have decided on a shadow show as our 'big production number', how is it best to approach the making of the cast? The BP *Puppet Company* topic favours a problem-solving approach to the making of puppets. To begin with, children are simply given a load of materials and told to 'make a puppet'. Then gradually, by constant re-assessment and refinement, they should arrive at a design which does what it should do and looks good. If you have enough time, this is an excellent way to proceed. I found that I wanted to 'feed in' information at various points during the process – and the best way was to present an example of the *wayang kulit* figures, or any other traditional shadow figure. If you do show a *wayang kulit* figure on your screen and ask children to examine it closely, you should elicit the following observations, which are absolutely essential if you are to make puppets which are usable later:

Firstly, the *wayang kulit* figure is reasonably large – and that is the first point to make. I find the utmost difficulty, whatever the age group, in persuading people to make their puppets *big*. And if they do not make them big enough, jointing becomes a real problem, as does visibility. The beauty of making puppetry your topic is that you give yourself the time to make mistakes and go back and improve your work, so that by the time you are ready to make the puppets for your final show the children should be really confident and able to relax and put their energy into making good characters.

Secondly, the joints of the *wayang kulit* are rounded. Although this may sound obvious, it is amazing how many people cut joints straight across and then wonder why their character has odd pointed bits sticking out whenever he bends his arm.

Thirdly, when the *wayang kulit* moves it does so in a wonderfully fluid way, as leather glides against leather, joined by smooth gut thread. And it is surprising, given the coarseness of the materials in comparison, how smooth a movement you can get from a puppet made out of card with a split-pin paper fastener as its joint, provided you punch a large enough hole so that the pin fits as loosely as possible.

At the same time as you are experimenting with your puppet-making, you can be choosing a story and preparing your play. The choice of story, and the methods of scripting and organisation into performance groups, are dealt with in Chapter 4.

As the term proceeds and you spend more and more time on rehearsal, you will want a number of relevant activities for those children not directly involved in the performance of the play. It is at this stage that the great variety of Language and Expressive Art activities thrown up by the *Puppet Company* topic really come into their own. It is a good idea to put up a large world map at the start and use it to locate the various countries where there is a puppetry tradition. This can lead into mapping work, and functional writing can then arise naturally from it. Instruction writing comes very naturally out of all kinds of practical activities associated with the topic. Ranjit, the Technology wizard, was poor at written language and his limited English vocabulary made functional writing a real nightmare. With help from an ESL (English as an additional language) teacher, he took his Technology ideas and painstakingly wrote them out – then read them back and altered them under her guidance, adding new words and expressions to make their meaning clearer. And because he was motivated by the need to spread his good idea, he stuck at a task which he would surely have abandoned had it been purely theoretical. In the end, he compiled a booklet of puppet-making instructions, which he collated himself and sold – the proceeds being used to buy some silver paint and a bag of wobbly eyes!

Designing a programme brings in some taxing language skills too: writing summaries is always difficult for children, and they have to sum up the story of the play in a couple of short paragraphs, leaving the ending up in the air to build up the audience's tension. Designing a programme brings in word-processing skills, too, and it is rewarding for everyone to see their name on the cast list or as 'lighting', 'sound' or whatever. In a large class it is not always easy to make sure that everyone has a part to play which they perceive as important, but there are various ways round this, discussed in detail in Chapter 4.

You will also want to have the children design posters and invitations – which also requires word-processing skills. There should be discussion about what information needs to be included and how it is best positioned, and it is good to do this on the computer so that different layouts can be tried out. For large full-colour posters it is a good exercise for children to do their own printing and think carefully about how it is best laid out. A4 flyers can be designed on the computer and a paste-up design run off on the photocopier.

Then there is the inevitable letter writing – formal letters to schools or community groups offering a performance of the show and giving precise details of the performance and the audience (age group and also number) it is suitable for; also the cost, space and facilities needed. All these details are crucial to the smooth running of the show, and children do not see this as an 'exercise' because it is *real* and about something they have an investment in.

The organisation of a 'tour' is the culmination of the term's work and is quite an operation. Buses have to be arranged, and the 'accountant' has to work out what price the tickets will have to be if they are to cover the expense of the

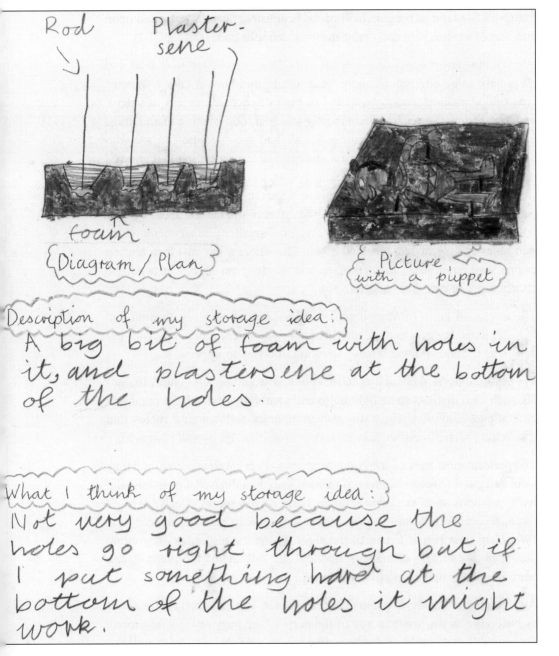

Rod   Plaster-
       sene

foam
{Diagram / Plan}

{Picture
with a puppet}

Description of my storage idea:
A big bit of foam with holes in
it, and plastersene at the bottom
of the holes.

What I think of my storage idea:
Not very good because the
holes go right through but if
I put something hard at the
bottom of the holes it might
work.

Figure 22: 'storage and transportation of puppets' idea

transport. Sometimes the goodwill of the headteacher can be prevailed upon and part of the bus hire costs paid from the school's budget.

When taking any production out of school, nothing can be left to chance, and there have to be discussions about what to take and how to take it. When I first started making shadow puppets I had not discovered the joys of Velcro, and our shadow figures had permanently attached rods, making them almost impossible to pack for transporting. So we had a competition to see who could come up with the best idea for storage and transportation that ensured that the puppets would always remain flat and not get rained upon if the weather was against us. Unsurprisingly, it was Ranjit who came up with the best design: an intricate affair composed of ever-smaller cardboard boxes with holes in them to carry each character, the smaller puppets being stuck into holes in the smallest box, and so on. The whole affair was then housed in one very large box – painted black and sporting our logo – to which he attached strong carrying handles.

There were all kinds of other ingenious ideas, one of which is illustrated in Fig. 22. It can be seen that the child herself was not entirely happy with her design as it stood and was already thinking of a way to improve it.

The children devised checklists so that nothing would be left behind, including such vital items as spare light bulbs and plenty of 'first aid' equipment in case of puppet injuries. There was also an itinerary, following the theory that it is better to have a master plan to deviate from than no overall plan at all.

The performances the children gave were always very well received, and they were delighted to receive letters of thanks. They had devised a questionnaire with questions such as 'What did you think of the sound effects? Why?'; 'Were the speakers clear? Why?'; 'What story would you like to see?' and 'What was your favourite part of the play?' Using the responses, they wrote their own assessments of the performance – the only really foolproof way to learn if a play works being to perform it.

As I pointed out at the beginning of the chapter, you can spend as much or as little time as you wish on any of the parts of the *Puppet Company* topic. You could, for example, make a shadow screen yourself and cut out all the Design Process work involved in the children's making it, leaving more time to concentrate on play writing. That is the beauty of it – no two *Puppet Company* topics will ever be the same.

The main advantage of the *Puppet Company* topic is the teamwork it engenders. Whether a child has a main puppeteering role or whether s/he only has to crash a cymbal to mark the death of a demon, every part is vital

9.00   COME into the School. Get your shoes On.
        Get the puppets ready. Then pack up the puppet booth
        Into the minibus (look at the checklist.)
9.30   Load the minibus. The minibus leaves School.

10.00   We arrive at the Rotary centre. We Will unload the minibus
        Set up the puppet Show.
10.30   The Audience arrives.
10.45   Perform puppet play.
11.00   Refreshments. Take down puppet booth and pack puppets.
        Load the minibus.
12.00   Return to school.

Figure 23: 'itinerary' idea

to the overall production. So many different talents come into play in the course of the topic, and I am always amazed by unexpected insights from unexpected children, sometimes in 'emergency' situations.

While most topics tend to 'dip' in the middle of the term and it is sometimes difficult to keep up enthusiasm, I never found this to be the case with the *Puppet Company*. There was always the goal of the performance in the distance and most of the work went towards attaining that goal.

I have always found that older children love reading to younger ones – particularly if they have written and illustrated the story themselves – and have often had older children regularly reading picture books to infants. Puppet performance is one stage further on – it allows the older children to share their creativity with the infants in a most satisfactory way, because it really is 'all their own work'.

3

Making puppets and screens

The two kinds of shadow puppet I use I call 'silhouette-style' and 'translucent'. Silhouette-style puppets are what most people think of when they hear the term 'shadow puppet'. They are cut out of black card, like those of Lotte Reiniger, and their charm and meaning lies in their outline. I use this type most commonly, and because I am fascinated by colour and its possibilities I tend to encourage children to cut pieces out of their figures and fill the shapes with coloured gels, cellophane or tissue paper.

'Translucent' puppets are cut out in the same way but require less emphasis on outline because the figures are drawn onto thin white card and coloured with water-based felt pens, so all kinds of details can be added. The card is rendered translucent by rubbing with vegetable oil after the colours have been applied.

It is surprising that the silhouette puppets are regarded as 'standard' – perhaps this is because the shadow puppets that were popular in Britain were the *ombres chinoises*. In fact the translucent puppets are nearer to the original Eastern ones and it is possible, using subtle colours and a great deal of patience, to mimic the Karagöz or *wayang kulit* forms quite effectively (*see* Photograph 1).

Silhouette-style puppets have certain advantages:

> *Aesthetic appeal*: To create the real magic of shadow theatre I think silhouette-style puppets are best. They are much more 'forgiving', so children with little artistic ability are amazed at the effectiveness of their figures. Colour gives them a wonderful 'stained glass' appearance, and all kinds of textures can be employed – lace, paper doilies, feathers, wool, wire, even pieces of leaf and wood – to create figures with extremely elaborate outlines.

Photograph 1: Translucent shadow puppets – Karagöz and Hacivat

Lighting: Silhouette-style shadow puppets can be shown on a screen with the aid of a simple anglepoise lamp in a room where the blackout is less than complete and still be very clear and effective. This is a very useful feature, particularly if you are going to show a play in a variety of venues, because you can not always be sure a room will be as dark as promised.

Backgrounds: With an overhead projector all kinds of good background effects can be created, as described later in this chapter. However, the backgrounds are really only effective with silhouette-style puppets because they tend to shine through the translucent figures and the effect is thus lost.

The main disadvantage with silhouette-style puppets is that I have to spend much of my workshop time cutting children's shapes out with a craft knife – hardly a tool for children. However, if you are making the puppets with your own class, you can make them in two stages. Ask the children to draw the shapes they would like to back with colour, cut them out later and use a second session to complete them. It is probably best to do this anyway, so the children can really concentrate on their designs in the first session.

Another solution is to supply the class with hole punches and suggest that they create patterns with them. Shadow figures such as fish look very good with patterns of dots covered in different colours. Another beautiful method of introducing colour which imitates the 'filigree' effect of the *wayang kulit* can be obtained with needles and a lump of plasticene. Swirling patterns, leaf and flower shapes etc. can be drawn on the figure with a pencil and then pricked out with different sizes of needles and pins. Needles can be a bit uncomfortable to work with like this, so set large darning needles into little dowel handles, creating your own tiny awls (*see* Photograph 2).

Translucent puppets have these advantages:

Detail: The teacher is not needed to cut out the details of clothes and features. These puppets are excellent for self-portraits.

Historical: As already mentioned, translucent puppets can 'imitate' the thin leather puppets of Indonesia, China, India and Turkey, and that would be my main reason for using them. The 'filigree' patterns can follow the lines of the coloured designs as described above, so that when the puppet is put on the shadow screen it really glows.

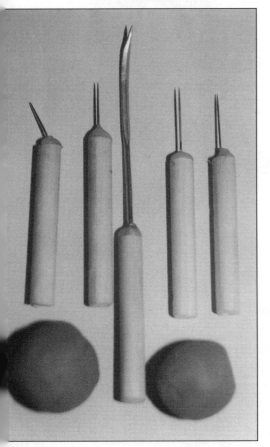

Illustrations – Translucent puppets are ideal for dramatising picture books where the characters are well-known to young children. For example, I have made translucent shadow figures from the illustrations in the picture-book *The Lighthouse Keeper's Lunch* (see Chapter 7).

Younger children: Translucent puppets can be made from young children's drawings and the effect is generally better than if you try to get them to reduce their ideas to a silhouette.

The disadvantages of the translucent puppets are that they do not work well in partial blackout; backgrounds are not as effective and, finally, they can be a bit messy. I always provide plenty of paper tissues and insist that puppet 'bits' are thoroughly dried off before they are put together and pressed against my shadow screen, but oily marks are inevitably left on it.

Photograph 2: 'Filigree' kit

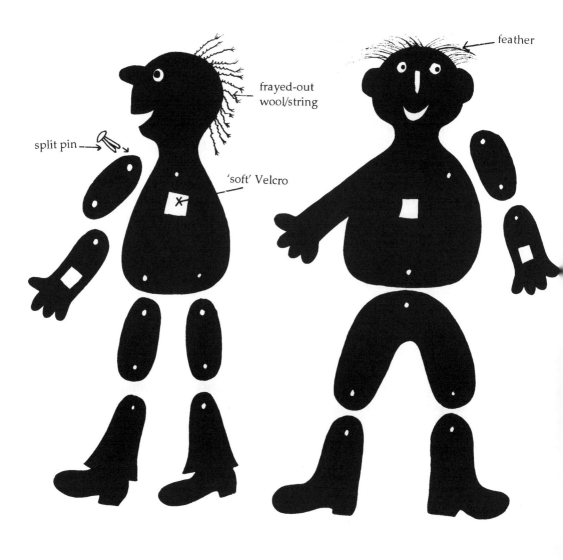

split pin

frayed-out
wool/string

'soft' Velcro

feather

Figure 24: Two methods of making human shadow puppets

It is for you to decide which kind of shadow puppet best fits your purpose. You will find instructions for making a human figure in profile or facing forward in Fig. 24.

There are two possible ways of jointing the legs. Both designs work well, but the one with a single 'hip' joint is possibly easier and could be further simplified for young children by omitting the knee joint. If you choose to make a profile figure you will not have to cut out features with a knife, but you do have to decide which way round it will need to face in performance. Various textures can be used for hair, and in animals for tails – frayed-out string or wool, feathers, and so on – and different kinds of textiles such as lace or gauze can make interesting clothes.

For really good movement, you can make the legs heavier either by attaching weights to the feet (metal washers are good) or making the legs the thickness of double card. This can make a big difference to the feel of the puppet, particularly if it has to do a lot of walking.

Instructions for puppet-making follow, and the chapter ends with descriptions of a variety of possible shadow screens. Your shadow screen should be already completed and in view when making the puppets because its size dictates the size of the puppets. Both children and adults tend to make their figures too small. I have tried all sorts of ways of cajoling them into drawing good-size figures but short of providing templates (which I dislike) it means constantly urging them to thicken up their shapes wherever necessary. Punching a hole somewhere on their scrap paper will show them how large the joints have to be. It helps to provide a sample puppet of good size and if time permits each child should have a chance to *use* it and get the feel of the size and the number of possible joints. And some traditional examples should if possible also be provided, to demonstrate size and roundness of joints as well as design and patterning.

Making a puppet

The children draw their designs on a large piece of scrap paper. The jointing can be discussed with each child as you go round the class. With beginners it is best to limit the number of 'controlled' joints (i.e. joints to which a rod will be attached) to two, though the legs can be jointed and move against the bottom ledge of the shadow screen without rod attachment. So for most animal characters you have the choice of moving a head, a jaw, a tail, or one of the limbs. Obviously when you are intending to use your figures to act out a play, the movements the character has to make will generally dictate which part you choose to move – crocodiles, for instance, lend themselves to huge snapping jaws.

If you want to provide an exercise in real cooperation, suggest that children work in pairs and produce shadow puppets which have to be operated by two people. Making them very large can produce fantastic puppets, such as dragons that move their heads up and down while swishing their tails and flapping their wings.

When the children have decided how the puppet should be jointed, the design should be re-drawn onto a piece of reasonably thick black card for a silhouette-type puppet and onto a piece of quite thin white card for a translucent one. The thinner the white card the better the colours show up when the oil is put on, but if you make the card too thin it is apt to tear easily, as oil makes card rather brittle. In general, if you are making translucent puppets for a performance you need to sacrifice some of the translucency in order to produce hard-wearing puppets.

Each piece which is to move separately has to be drawn separately. It is amazing how difficult this concept can be, even to not-so-young people, and if they can not grasp this it may be easier to leave them to work it out for themselves by trial and error.

In Fig. 25 are suggestions for the designs of characters for the play printed at the end of the chapter, *The Great Big Red Apple*.

If you want the head of your puppet to move, a good stout neck is essential, as in the elephant in Fig. 25. Without this neck, too much of the head will be lost in the overlapping. All joints need to be robust, and even an animal with slim legs can have quite sizeable joints – look at the rabbit in Fig. 25. Making 'swollen' joints like this looks more realistic, and the puppet will be much stronger. The design for the snake can be adapted for all sorts of animals – a swan, for example, can be given a beautifully long and sinuous neck by means of a series of circles, as can a giraffe.

If you punch or cut out a good-sized eye and back it with colour the effect can be rather dead. An easy way to bring expression to the puppet's face is to collect up the circles of card that fall out of the hole punch and stick them back on. Children like to play about with the different expressions this can produce.

At this point you need to ensure that all the pieces are a reasonable size. You also need to discuss quite fully beforehand how large each character should be in relation to the others, though it is all right to 'cheat' a bit. If you have an elephant and a mouse in the same play it is impossible to make them to the correct proportions!

Figure 25: Suggested designs for characters in The Great Big Red Apple

For translucent shadow puppets, the pieces are now ready to be coloured in with felt pens. I like to encourage people to use a fair amount of black, in eyes and other features (you could remind the children about old Karagöz's vanity and how he thought his 'black eye' was a sign of beauty). Black outlines also help to define figures on the screen. Remember to leave the *white* of the eye uncoloured to give the puppet life.

The pieces should be cut out carefully, making sure with the translucent puppets that you do not lose the black outline. Leave a narrow white edge all round if possible. For silhouette-style puppets I like to provide a variety of scissors so that fancy edges can be cut. Next, holes should be punched for the joints. The holes need to be large enough to let the paper fasteners move very freely. Use the largest hole on a variable-hole punch, and don't punch them too near the edge of the card or they will rip.

The coloured puppet pieces can now be made translucent. If you begin by rubbing the oil into the white side, you can see the colours appearing and this gives an indication of when to stop applying oil. You can rub oil in from either side though – the colours will not run. Encourage the children to keep holding the shapes up to the light to check on their translucency. Incidentally, this is an excellent way to teach a difficult word – even very young children can say it by the end of a workshop, and older classes can compare the terms 'translucent' and 'transparent'.

After drying off any excess oil, insert the split-pin paper fasteners. You can buy 'micro' paper fasteners which have tiny 'arms' from art shops. These are wonderful but pretty expensive to provide for a whole class, so I tend to go for the standard school issue ones, even though their arms are nearly 2 cm long so they stick out and break up the outline. The answer is to bend them back on themselves, and they may obligingly snap off when you do so, leaving arms just the right length. Do not tighten the paper fasteners at this stage – particularly not in the leg joints. You want a puppet whose legs move freely so that you get optimal movement.

Shapes can now be cut out of the silhouette-type puppets and the spaces backed with cellophane. For special puppets I use gels produced for stage lighting, which are available from theatre stockists in every colour under the sun. These are so strong that you can cut out large areas of card and then create lovely effects by overlapping colour upon colour. They are quite expensive but worth it for a special performance, and they have wonderful names like 'gaslight green', 'surprise blue', 'rose gold' and, my favourite, 'dark bastard amber'!

Photograph 3: Silhouette-style shadow puppet – Cuthbertson Primary, Glasgow.

Normally, though, I provide ordinary cellophane, which I cut into very small pieces to avoid waste. If the pieces are small it encourages children to try mixing, which gives more interesting effects than plain colour. At this stage other textures can also be experimented with, either on their own or in conjunction with cellophane – a paper doily backed with red cellophane, for example, makes a lovely ballgown for Cinderella.

Photograph 4: Silhouette-style shadow puppet – Cuthbertson Primary, Glasgow.

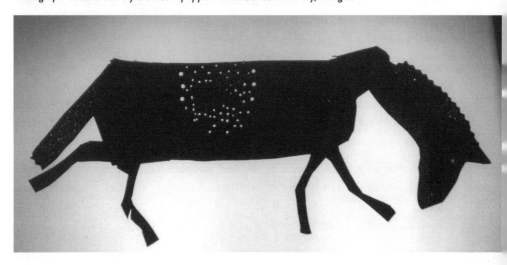

Two examples of silhouette-style shadow puppets are shown in photographs 3 and 4, each showing the effect of 'filigree-work'. The puppets were made by children aged 7-8.

Once all the pieces are completed, it is time to attach rods. This can be done in different ways. For silhouette-type puppets I used to use garden rods or kebab skewers attached at right angles to the puppet with strong carpet tape. This is quick and quite easy but leaves you with a set of about thirty objects that look like little porcupines and are impossible to store! And it is unsatisfactory for translucent puppets because no adhesive adheres to oiled card for long so the tape has to be stapled on. Velcro is the answer. I glue the 'rough' side of the Velcro firmly onto the rods with hot-melt glue, and staple a small piece of the 'soft' Velcro onto the back of the puppet. If care is taken when detaching the rods (hold the soft Velcro as you do it) this will last for ages. Puppets can be stored in folders, or even stuck on the window as a display.

Rods should ideally be made of wire with wooden dowel handles as in Fig. 26, the 'de luxe' wire rod. The longer they are the more awkward they are to use, but the more of the screen you can cover without the shadow of your hands appearing. Normally I would make rods about 35 cm long for children, but if you want a character like a bird or a tall giraffe to have full freedom to move around the screen, you can provide rods of 50 cm or more.

Wire rods with handles take a little time to prepare but you only need about ten for most productions, and the shadow cast by fine wire is beautifully discreet. Either glue on two 'rough' Velcro squares as shown, or glue on just one square and fold it over on itself. You can make 'cheapy' rods by gluing the Velcro onto the tip of a stout green garden stick. That takes less time and is a bit cheaper, but it casts a much thicker shadow and is inflexible. Also the squares do have a tendency to come off – so carry spares! For very young children I make chunky rods of dowel which they find easy to hold and operate.

Note that, unlike the *wayang kulit* figures, these shadow puppets are operated by rods held *horizontally* – at an angle to the screen. This gives a much crisper outline than if they were held vertically, which only works well on screens without frames – stretched silk or cotton sheets like the traditional screens.

When attaching the soft Velcro to their puppets, children often ask where they should place it. I try not to tell them but rather discuss it and let them decide. It is really a problem of levers and centres of gravity, and too good a teaching point to be missed unless you are very pushed for time.

'de luxe' wire rod

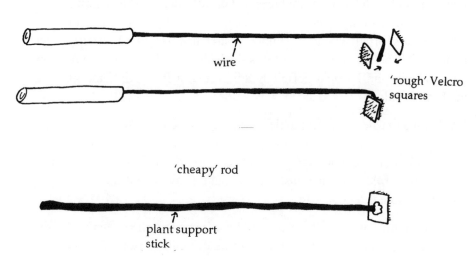

wire

'rough' Velcro
squares

'cheapy' rod

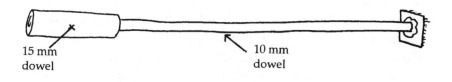

plant support
stick

'infant' rod

15 mm
dowel

10 mm
dowel

... and the rods in use!

Figure 26: Rod designs

Next we come to the screen. Screens can be made from a number of different materials and each has its advantages and disadvantages. The nearest screen to the traditional one is the cotton screen. As I said before, the traditional *wayang kulit* arrangement is simply a stretched length of material and puppets are applied vertically, but it is difficult to find attachment points in most schools and I would definitely advise that a frame of some kind be made or found.

Fig 27a shows a design for a simple cotton shadow screen. The frame is made out of 2 cm X 2 cm wood (don't buy very cheap pine because it is bound to warp) with right angle brackets at the inside corners. These screens must not be too large or they become unstable – about one and a half metres long by one metre wide is a good size.

You can simply nail or tack the cotton to the frame, but the cotton will soon loosen and get dirty, and the screen will be difficult to store. Far better to spend an evening sewing the soft side of Velcro round the sides of the hemmed cotton, then nail the rough side to the screen as shown. The best nails for this are those designed for use in cabinetmaking, because the nails must be short so that they do not go right through the frame, thin so that they do not split the wood, and their heads must be relatively large so that they do not slip back through the Velcro. If you position your Velcro carefully so that you get a really good 'stretch' you can dismantle the screen after each performance, wash it if necessary, and store it easily in a plastic bag ready to be newly-stretched next time. And the frame itself can be hung up out of the way where it won't annoy the janitor.

Fig. 27b shows the screen in use with an overhead projector. Alternative lighting arrangements are anglepoise lamps sitting on the floor or on a table, or clip-on lamps attached to the top of the frame, which are far safer. Using two light sources can pose a problem because if the beams cross they cause multiple shadows so must be carefully adjusted. Their advantage is that you can control each separately, switching off one to dim half the screen, or putting a filter over just one.

It is best not to have any child operating shadow puppets for too long because even with cushions to kneel on it can become quite uncomfortable. The solution is to build a big free-standing screen as in Fig. 27c.

A free-standing screen as shown on page 59 is much more substantial but also harder to store and transport. In discussions with your class (as suggested in Chapter 2), 'portability' will have been acknowledged as important, so the legs need to be made separately. The higher you make your

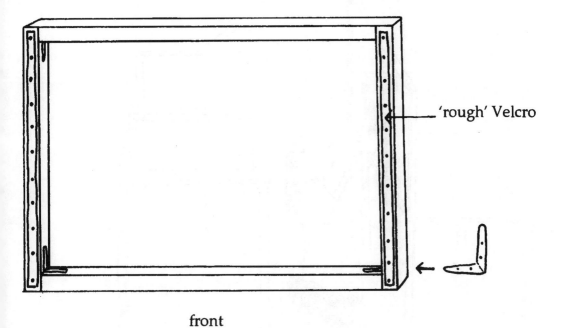

'rough' Velcro

front

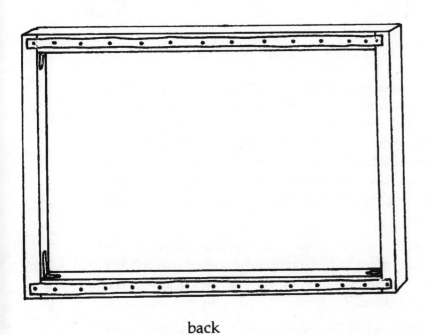

back

Figure 27a: Design for frame for cotton screen

Figure 27b: Cotton shadow screen in use with OHP

screen, the wobblier it becomes, so it may be best if the puppeteers agree that they will sit or kneel. Moreover, if you want to use a free-standing light or overhead projector, a high screen is a problem as your light source should be higher than your screen. Expensive overhead projectors wobbling about on high trolleys are nerve-wracking, and it is difficult and dangerous to change scenes on them, so you have to compromise. The puppeteers could sit on chairs rather than standing so that they are not so tall. This is comfortable but limits their movements.

A different type of shadow screen can be made from clear Perspex backed with good quality tracing paper. I like the effect these screens give, and they are good to work on, but Perspex is rather expensive and difficult to cut and drill. It is also difficult to store.

Finally, the photographs 5, 6 and 7 on page 60 show a small desktop screen I use in schools. It is made of Perspex and is easily transportable with its screw-off feet. As Photograph 7 shows, I have given the screen a slight forward tilt by sticking two little blocks of wood to the end of the feet at the

58

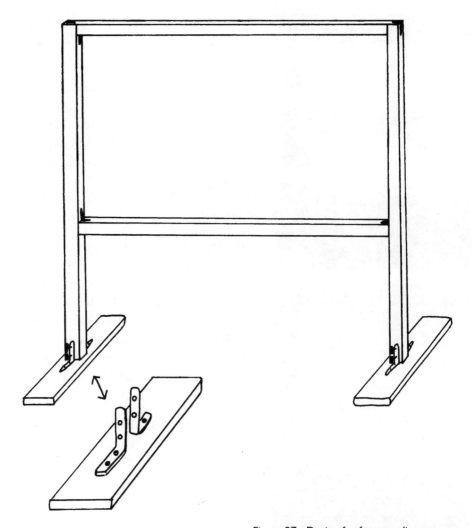

Figure 27c: Design for free-standing screen

'operator' side. Each block is backed with felt to make it 'non-slip'. This makes using scenery somewhat easier because it will stay in place, and it is possible to 'rest' a puppet without it falling off. A large piece of thick rubber foam on the tabletop behind the screen allows the puppets to rest in a chosen position with its rods – one advantage of tabletop work.

Your screen will have a ledge on which you can make the puppets walk, but it is useful also to provide a slit or two to hold scenery and prop items, as in the play that follows, where an apple tree with its enormous fruit has to be visible throughout. An overhead projector allows for the creation of lovely backgrounds from a few dry grasses, heathers, and other vegetation collected

and arranged on its screen. Fig. 28 shows a few ideas.

Once you get started, all sorts of ideas will emerge about ways to make puppets and screens, ideas generated by your own needs and circumstances and, of course, by the children. A good book offering lots of clearly-illustrated practical ideas on shadow puppetry is *Worlds of Shadow* by David and Donna Wisniewski (see *Further Reading*).

The sample play which ends this chapter, *The Great Big Red Apple*, is suitable for eight to ten years olds to perform for an audience of younger children. There is a good deal of repetition, which also makes it suitable for the class to read before writing their own play. And it's a great way of practising superlatives!

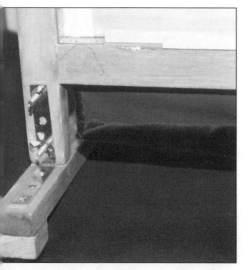

Top left: Photograph 5: Small Perspex screen – audience side

Middle: Photograph 6: Small Perspex screen – operator side

Left: Photograph 7: Small perspex screen to show ledge for props, and blocks under feet to angle screen forward

Landscape created from dried grasses, leaves etc.

'Cave' using black card cut-outs backed with coloured cellophane, with dried grasses

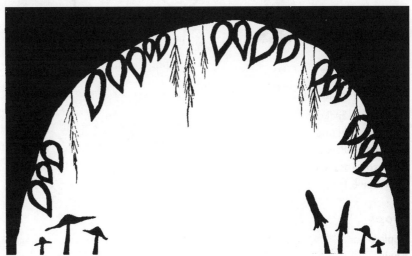

Landscape created from cut-out cellophane pieces

Figure 28: Some methods of creating backgrounds using the OHP screen

The Great Big Red Apple
a play for shadow puppets

Cast

Narrator 1 Elephant
Narrator 2 Snake
Narrator 3 Hippo
Narrator 4 Parrot
Narrator 5 Rabbit
Narrator 6 Mouse

Props

Apple tree
Apple
Core
Red filter
Blue filter

Narrator 1   In the middle of a forest grew an apple tree ...

Narrator 2   ... and in the middle of the apple tree, all big and red and shiny ...

Narrator 3   ... grew an apple. Just one big, red, shiny apple.

Narrator 4   It was the biggest, reddest, shiniest apple you have ever seen ...

Narrator 5   ... and it looked just ready to eat!

Narrator 6   An elephant came along, and when she saw the apple she said ...

Elephant Good gracious me! What a wonderful apple! I would *love* to eat that apple!

Narrator 1 The elephant tried and tried to reach the apple.

Narrator 2 She tried to stretch her trunk to pull it off the tree, but it was just too high.

Narrator 3 She tried standing on tiptoe, but still she wasn't tall enough.

Narrator 4 She tried shaking the trunk with her own trunk, but that didn't work.

Narrator 5	She tried kicking the tree, but *that* didn't work.
Narrator 6	She even tried jumping, but she wasn't really a very good jumper – so that didn't work either.

Then along came a snake ...

Snake	(*looking at the apple*) Well, bless my soul! What a big, juicy-looking apple! I would love to have it, but I know I can't reach it.
Narrator 1	The snake tried to climb the apple tree, but its trunk was very slippy and he kept falling back down.
Narrator 2	He tried a few times, but every time he fell in a heap on the ground.
Narrator 3	And at last he crawled away, saying ...
Snake	I don't want the silly apple anyway. I bet it's sour.
Narrator 4	The elephant tried to stretch up again, but still she couldn't reach the apple.
Narrator 5	She looked up at it longingly.
Narrator 6	She was quite sure the apple *wasn't* sour! Then along came a hippo. He looked up at the apple and he said ...
Hippo	(*looking at the apple*) Gosh – what a whopper! I've never, in my whole life, seen such a big apple. Oh – what a lovely snack it would be!

Narrator 1	The hippo took three steps backwards, and then he charged at the tree trunk.
Narrator 2	The tree gave a little wobble, but the apple stayed exactly where it was.
Narrator 3	He tried again, and again, and again – but the apple was stuck fast. At last he stomped off, grumbling ...
Hippo	I never really wanted the stupid apple. It's probably so hard it would give me tummy-ache!

Narrator 4   The elephant gave the tree another little push, but of course the apple stayed just where it was.

Narrator 5   She looked at it even more longingly than before.

Narrator 6   She was absolutely sure that the apple wouldn't give *her* tummy-ache!

Then there was a fluttering sound from above her head, and a parrot landed on the top of the tree.

She gave the apple a little push with her beak and she said ...

Parrot   Wowee! This is the best apple I have ever seen. I could feed my three chicks on this and still have lots left for myself.

But the stalk looks so tough – I'm sure I won't be able to get it off the tree.

Narrator 1   The parrot pecked and pecked at the stalk.

Narrator 2   She pecked till her head hurt, but still the apple didn't budge.

Narrator 3   She pecked till she was worried that her beak would go blunt, but still the apple didn't budge. At last she flew off, squawking ...

Parrot   Only a fool would want to eat such a big apple. Everyone knows that big apples are tasteless!

Narrator 4   The elephant tried another jump, but of course it was no good. She was nowhere near the big shiny apple.

Narrator 5   She stared and stared at it, wishing it would drop down at her feet.

Narrator 6   She was quite, quite sure that the apple was as tasty as it was big.

Then she heard a nervous little cough from the other side of the tree and she looked round the trunk. There was a rabbit, looking up at the apple.

Rabbit   Oh me! Oh my! Oh me! Oh my! Oh me! Oh my!

Elephant   Oh dear me! Calm down, Rabbit – haven't you ever seen an apple before?

Rabbit   Not such a great big enormous one, I haven't! It's colossal! Why – it would feed my brothers and my sisters and my cousins and my babies and my husband – and there would still be something left for me!

Narrator 1   The rabbit tried to climb the tree, but she couldn't.

Narrator 2   She tried to jump up into the branches, but she couldn't.

Narrator 3   She even tried running at the trunk and pushing it with her head, but of course nothing happened. At last she went right up to the elephant and she said, very shyly ...

Rabbit   I have an idea, Elephant.

Elephant   And what might that be, little Rabbit?

Rabbit   If I jumped up on your back, oh mighty Elephant, and I climbed right up on to your trunk, oh great Elephant, and I stretched up as high as I could, oh great *and* mighty Elephant – then ...

Elephant	My trunk would be so strained that it would probably never work properly again. No, little Rabbit – that is not a good idea.
Rabbit	Oh no – *dear* Elephant! I am so light, honestly – I won't harm your great trunk, I promise. Please let me climb up on your back!
Elephant	No! Absolutely *not!* I mean to say – if I have to share the apple with you, and your husband, and your whole family, how much will *I* get? It won't be worth it!
Narrator 4	They argued, and they argued, and they argued.
Narrator 5	The sun set, and all the forest turned red in its light – and still they argued. (*red filter*)
Narrator 6	The sun went down, (*blue filter*) and the forest went to sleep, and still they argued. (*blackout*)
	They argued all night, and in the morning ...
	(*Lights on, to show the tree with just a core*)
	... when they looked up they saw, to their horror, that nothing was left of the great big red apple but a core.
Elephant	Oh no! Our apple has gone!
Rabbit	Oh my! Oh me! Oh my! Oh me! What can have happened?
Narrator 1	And then, out from the leaves of the apple tree there crawled a little mouse ...

Narrator 2   ... a very *full* little mouse ...

Narrator 3   ... a little mouse who could hardly crawl because his tummy was so full ...

Narrator 4   ... a little mouse who could hardly crawl because his tummy was so full of apple ...

Narrator 5	... a little mouse who could hardly crawl because his tummy was so full of ...
Narrators 1-6	... THE GREAT BIG RED APPLE!!!
Narrator 1	So the elephant looked at the rabbit ...
Narrator 2	... and the rabbit looked at the elephant ...
Narrator 3	... and they both said ...
Elephant and Rabbit	It wasn't *that* good an apple *anyway*!
Narrator 4	And they both went home.
Narrator 5	And the little mouse lay down under the apple tree ...
Narrator 6	... and before he went back to sleep he said ...
Mouse	That was the biggest, reddest, tastiest, ripest, juiciest apple I have *ever* eaten!

Song of the Animals
To the tune of 'What Shall We Do With The Drunken Sailor?'

Who ate the apple? Not the snake!
Who ate the apple? Not the snake!
Who ate the apple? Not the snake -
'Cause he couldn't climb up!

Chorus: *Hey! Ho! A great big apple*
             Oh my! A big red apple
             Hey! Ho! I'd love to eat it
             Early in the morning!

Who ate the apple? Not the hippo!
Who ate the apple? Not the hippo!
Who ate the apple? Not the hippo -
'Cause he couldn't push it!

Chorus

Who ate the apple? Not the parrot!
Who ate the apple? Not the parrot!
Who ate the apple? Not the parrot -
'Cause she couldn't peck it!

Chorus

Who ate the apple? Yes – the mouse did!
Who ate the apple? Yes – the mouse did!
Who ate the apple? Yes – the mouse did –
Early in the morning!

Chorus

4

Play writing and production

Your screen is ready, and your class has mastered the art of making shadow puppets. It is time to think about a suitable performance. How do you go about it?

The importance of audience awareness has already been signalled. That should be your starting point in any piece of written work and is particularly vital when you are planning a performance. There is nothing more disheartening for children than losing their audience's attention, which usually happens because the story doesn't come across clearly. It is extremely difficult to convey to older children how careful they have to be in terms of setting the scene and introducing the characters in any story for a younger audience, yet this is surely *the* art of true story-telling.

If you are intending to put on a play for seven year olds, say, the first thing to do is to look at the books this class is reading and to give your class a chance to read to the younger ones. Then you can discuss the elements that make a good story – what did the younger children like? What did they react well to? Usually there is plenty of repetition in stories for young children; in fairy tales lines are repeated over and over again until the children find themselves joining in. This is excellent for a puppet play; it ensures that you don't lose your audience, because you are constantly repeating a plot line and involving them in the story.

The other important area where stories frequently fall down is in character development. Children often assume that because *they* know their monkey is called Nicky and is very naughty, everyone else knows too. And in a puppet play with many different characters, things can become hopelessly confusing for the audience if characters are not introduced properly. When a character appears, either it has to say its name or someone else must say it. So in a play for young children there have to be lines like 'Oh hello Nicky! Have you been up to any of your tricks today?'.

One way of ensuring that a character is well and truly understood is to invent a little catchphrase for it. The most common device, which children just love to do, is to have it say something like, 'Hello boys and girls – my name's Nicky the Monkey. Can you say 'hello' to me? Let's try ...' and so on, egging on the audience with 'I can't hear you – louder!' This ensures that the audience is never lost for long; as soon as the character appears they are instantly engaged.

The device of speaking directly to the audience works less well with shadow puppets because of the lack of direct contact with the audience. One solution is to use a rod or glove puppet as your 'link'. This can be extremely effective and it gives the extraverts opportunities to display their talents. For example, you could have a rod or glove puppet who is a wizard and who invites the children to 'watch his magic screen' (see Chapter 5). If he appears at the beginning of each scene, he helps the audience to follow the plot of the shadow play, saying things like, 'I wonder what will happen next, boys and girls? Let's find out!'

You may choose to dramatise a story which you know appeals to the children. If the book it is in is well illustrated, it will be particularly effective. Although this may be considered 'copying', it practises a range of important skills and ensures that the play has a storyline familiar to the audience. Look for stories which don't have too many characters and where the characters are well developed.

Or you may prefer to write your own material. This is fraught with problems because if you give the class free rein you will be presented with thirty stories, many of which will be quite unsuitable, however much time has been spent discussing the genre. I prefer to limit the task by having the class decide on the main storyline and then asking groups to write separate scenes, or by providing some kind of framework in which children each provide a small piece of dialogue to fit a given situation.

For example in *The Great Big Red Apple*, you could start by discussing the overall 'plot' – that an elephant finds an apple tree with one great big apple which he can't reach – and develop a storyline in discussion with the class. Who might come along? What might that character say? What strategies could that character use for getting the apple down? Once you have discussed four or five animals' reactions, children can be set the task of writing out the conversations between each animal and the elephant, according to a pattern you have decided upon. In that way each child or group of children contributes to the overall play, but a pattern is assured.

Another good storyline is 'the princess who would not laugh'. This is a scenario with which most children will be familiar; the king sends far and wide for people to come and try to make his daughter laugh and so earn her hand in marriage. In groups, children have to decide who will visit the princess, what they will do to amuse her, and what the reaction will be. This is a particularly good scenario because almost anything goes in terms of characters and acts. And if you want to break the sexist fairy tale mould, you could have your princess decide in the end that she would rather not marry any of her suitors. Once you start to break down stories into little scenes in this way, it becomes easier to envisage performances and it also means you have discrete units for rehearsal.

Or you can base the show on a theme and write poems or short prose pieces around it (described in more detail in Chapter 5). Some long poems and songs lend themselves well to shadow presentations too, and no original writing is required. Instead, time can be spent devising effective ways of interpreting the poet's words, perhaps adding music. Shadow theatre is such a lyrical medium that it lends itself to highly descriptive presentations and all kinds of special effects to create moods, some of which are described later in the chapter. You do not even need to use words at all – if your puppets are expressive enough and the children perform well, they can effectively interpret music from, for instance, Saint-Saëns' *Carnival of the Animals*.

When discussing potential material, it is crucial to develop in older children the faculty of looking critically at content. Publishers are much more careful these days, but there are still stories going about which have doubtful attitudes to race, religion and gender. If you do find a story which is, for example, sexist – and many fairy tales are quite painfully so – this can be a useful starting point for discussion. Changing the sexes of the characters in a traditional story can be fun and also most 'educational'. I remember a hilarious puppet production based on the story of Snow White, in which a beautiful young *boy* finds a cottage where seven women live. Every morning they go off to work in the city with their word-processors, leaving him to do the housework. Stereotypes exist to be challenged – men can cry and women can save the day!

Similarly, children should be aware of racism in stories they read – which can be extremely subtle. Are there stereotyped black characters in the story? Are there statements which could be insulting to certain people? Are all the characters white? Discussions about such matters often arise out of common assumptions which are still made in stories: Sunday is the holy day, Christmas is celebrated, we all go to church, and so on. I think it is essential, particularly in all-white schools, that children are aware that this is not necessarily the norm for everyone in society, so that when they write a play they can just as readily decide that it is Friday and Sameera is going to the mosque.

This is a sensitive issue and requires careful treatment. All too often I have seen performances where 'ethnic minority' characters have been included to give the puppet company a 'multicultural' outlook, but where these characters are developed with little actual knowledge and sensitivity they become token figures, included *because* of their ethnic origins and not because of their inherent qualities and worth in the story. Other matters for discussion might include whether *The Three Little Pigs* would be an appropriate story for adaptation if there are Muslim children in the audience.

Finally, another way of discussing ideas for productions and writing a play is to start with the puppets. Ask the children to invent a character – human, animal or 'extra-terrestrial' – sketch it and make it as a shadow puppet. Next they write a 'puppet profile' of their character: its name and where it lives, what kind of character it is, and so on. You can help by providing possible adjectives such as 'shy', 'happy', 'optimistic', 'nervous' etc. When they have a clear picture of what their character is like, the children put him/her on the screen and answer questions from the teacher, which are very basic: 'What's your name?', 'Where do you live?' What do you eat?' and 'Have you got a family?' The 'rule' of this improvisation game is that no-one is ever allowed to say 'I don't know'! So anything the children have not worked out in advance they will have to make up as they go along. This elicits amusing character profiles and it gives the children a chance to think about what kind of voice their character would use and how it would speak.

Once the basic information is established I invite the other children to ask questions which would help in building up a detailed picture of the character. In this way stories can begin to form quite naturally. If, for example, someone has made a lion who is afraid of mice, and someone else has made a mouse who isn't afraid of anything, you have the basis of a plot. Usually at the end of an improvisation session the class splits into small groups with puppets that have something in common, and they can begin to put their ideas down on paper. I would certainly hope to get more than one play out of a session like this – the chances of being able to work twenty-odd characters into any kind of story is extremely slim.

Having decided on your story, puppet production can begin. I would strongly advise that you allow the children to make a 'practice' puppet first so that all the usual mistakes can be made on a figure that does not matter. If you are going to work on a single 'class' production it is probably better to let children work in pairs so that everyone feels they have contributed. Or split the class into 'makers' and 'writers', so that your script is being produced at the same time as the puppet characters.

If you are working from a published story, it is a good idea, and also more fun than straightforward writing, first to construct 'storyboards'. This is like drawing cartoons and lends itself particularly well to the production of a shadow puppet play (which is a form of animated cartoon). This involves a good deal of decision making and is best led by a teacher. Discuss what the main points in the story are and then illustrate them, writing the lines spoken underneath or in 'bubbles'. This will indicate what backgrounds will be needed, and how characters will make their entrances. If you are doing this alongside the puppet-makers, you will be on hand to tell them what direction each puppet must be made to face – always an important decision.

Using speech bubbles is a good way of teaching older children the conventions of punctuating direct speech. Stage directions such as 'quietly' provide good models for sentences like, *'I have an idea,' said Rabbit quietly*. This is an interesting way of working, because you are starting with the 'play' form and using it to help write a story.

I would always advocate classes writing their own material, but should you decide to put on *The Great Big Red Apple* rather than write your own this is still a valid exercise. Different skills are involved in following a script and making someone else's characters. It is much easier to be told to 'make an animal shadow puppet' than to 'make an *elephant* shadow puppet', and to have to follow prescribed lines and stage instructions is not easy either.

The play can also be used to read with the children as a stimulus to discussion of the genre. I have taken care that there are hardly ever more than two characters on screen at any time – and that is a crucial point to make. There are also few props and only one slight scene change. It is better to perform something very simple and perform it well, than to go for a play which is too complex and works less well.

You could also use this play as a 'template' for your own invented characters. What would happen if a giraffe came along? Or a horse? And what other endings could there be? I use several narrators in the play, a device which is particularly good for shadow theatre, where you do not want too much action. The narrators' parts have been kept simple and repetitive so the play is suitable for a young audience and could even be performed by a very young class. And having many different narrators involves more children, and keeps each part short enough to memorise easily – which is an advantage in a theatre form that operates in the dark.

In Chapter 3 mention was made of possible backgrounds using the overhead projector screen (see Fig. 28) but care is needed not to clutter up the performance area as the puppets need room to move! The overhead projector screen allows for the creation of naturalistic scenery by drawing on acetates with the appropriate pens. These backgrounds are quite easy: trace over a drawing with the pens. But they can be fuzzy and indistinct. If the children have gels or cellophane and cut out shapes like trees, castles etc. which they glue onto the acetate, the glue can combine with the cellophane in interesting ways, such as blue sea with lovely watery textures in it. It is also possible to make a colour photocopy on acetate of a photograph, a picture or, best of all, a child's own artwork.

A sea voyage can be beautifully realised by moving a piece of blue cellophane slowly up and down on the overhead projector screen. And the co-ordination required to move a boat on the shadow screen in time to the movements of the sea makes it a wonderful exercise in cooperation.

If you have a roller on your overhead projector you can make backgrounds which can move. This can be a long continuous piece of scenery, or you can create a number of distinct scenes which run smoothly from one to the other. There are acetates suitable for computer printers which can be effectively used to display the title of a play at the beginning and perhaps a cast list or the words of a song at the end, giving a 'professional' look that children like.

Background items can be made out of card and laid directly against the shadow screen. By creating a narrow slit on the bottom ledge, as shown in Photograph 7, the scenery can be slotted in easily. If the scenery items are too high they will bend away from the screen. Other props can be hung from the top of the screen by thin thread.

The overhead projector screen may be used as a performing surface. Lay a fairly small puppet on it and move it so that its shadow appears on the shadow screen, very large and 'fuzzy'. This is good for a magical character: the audience first sees its shape looming over the screen as a huge shadow, then slowly it appears more and more clearly until it is right against the shadow screen.

Filters can be used with any lighting method and are most effective to create moods, temperatures, and times of day. Glue a large piece of cellophane of the desired colour onto a piece of rectangular card with its centre cut away. It should look like a TV screen, and be large enough to cover the overhead projector screen easily without showing its edges. Blue filters give the impression of cold, or loneliness, or evening. Following with orange or red filters suggests dawn breaking, the earth becoming warmer, and the character feeling happier again. Red filters also help signal a battle or a sudden magical spell. And for a *really* magical background, stick your cellophane onto a sheet of bubble-wrap and place it on the overhead projector screen – the effect is wonderful.

You can be adventurous and use trays of water on your overhead projector screen, floating objects or dyes on the surface, but there is the danger of the equipment getting soaked.

Involving the whole class

It is easier to find meaningful parts for everyone in shadow theatre than in conventional drama. There are so many little effects you can add which do not require enormous talent or great voice projection but which are nevertheless impressive. My first 'public performance' was a version of the creation myth of Hanuman the monkey god, in which the high point of the story is where Hanuman is hit by a thunderbolt and falls from the sky. The accompanying sound effect on an electronic keyboard was splendid, but only if sounded at exactly the right moment and for exactly the right time. So the child who provided it never felt that hers was a minor part. She had to practise hard to get it just right and was justifiably proud of the result.

Taking *The Great Big Red Apple* as an example then, and a class of thirty children, how does everyone get something important to do?

First of all, there are the puppeteers. Although everyone will want the chance to perform with the puppet they make, for an actual play there can be only a small group of puppeteers, determined by the size of your screen. I would have no more than three children at once behind an average 1.5 metre by 1 metre screen. *The Great Big Red Apple* allows for a different puppeteer for each animal that comes on to meet the elephant. The children have to sit quietly with their puppets at the ready and slide into position when it is their part, replacing the previous puppeteer. This gives parts for six puppeteers. One person without a puppet is needed in overall charge of things behind the screen – ideally someone clear-headed! And two people are needed to operate the lighting and filters. This gives parts for nine children.

In most forms of puppetry the person operating the puppet also provides its voice. In rod or glove puppetry the performance will be convincing only when the energy of the voice comes from the same source as the energy in the arm. In shadow puppetry too, movements coordinate better with voice if the puppeteer speaks. However, the advantage of shadow theatre is that it *can* work when some children provide the voices while others operate the puppets, particularly when there are narrators, and this makes the shadow play ideal for larger groups. *The Great Big Red Apple* has twelve speaking parts, so twenty one children already have something important to do.

The people who are providing the voices need not be concealed. If the puppetry is good the audience will be transfixed by what is happening on the screen, and it is far better that they hear the voices clearly. I would set out six chairs on either side of the screen, probably in two rows of three, for the 'voice' people.

There is usually at least one 'musician' in any class, and even if their musical prowess only stretches to selecting a variety of little tunes on an electronic keyboard, such music can be very effective if done properly. An interesting exercise, particularly if you have access to a music specialist, is to devise a simple melody or rhythm and then adapt it to fit a variety of characters. So the elephant could enter to very slow, deep music, and the tune be played higher and faster for smaller animals. Or use the same tune in different keys to show changes in mood. When the dying Hanuman was borne up to the sky by his father the Wind god, the jolly little tune we had picked out for him in life was played very slowly in a minor key while a blue filter was held in front of the lights.

If one person provides music, and another the sound effects like footsteps, crunching, etc. you have parts for twenty three, and the rest of the class could be grouped to the side as the choir for the final song. Or there could be a little 'orchestra' of simple instruments to provide sound effects and incidental music. Rainsticks are wonderful. These are hollowed-out pieces of branch into which cactus-spines have been stuck on the inside. Filled with seeds or small pebbles and inverted, they make a sound like rain falling or the sea washing on the shore. They are expensive to buy but can be made out of cardboard tubes. Insert toothpicks at intervals down the length of the tube, cutting off the part that sticks out and fixing with glue. Fill with beads or seeds and cover the whole thing with paper coloured to look like wood. You can experiment with different lengths and widths to get different tones.

Finally, the children with small parts can also take the tickets and show the audience to their seats.

Performance Skills

Plays must be well-rehearsed, but it is best to keep practice times quite short, 'little but often' being easier for all concerned. Over-rehearsing can be almost as bad as under-rehearsing, and it is best to stop while the children are still enthusiastic. In comparison to conventional drama, puppet plays are very short and it is easier to become mechanical and lose the initial sparkle.

Puppets should generally be held in gentle contact with the shadow screen in order to be seen clearly. This is less important with silhouette-style puppets but vital with translucent ones. Exits and entrances can be made by slowly removing the puppet or placing it so that it 'fades out' or appears gradually, but for *The Great Big Red Apple* each animal can walk, slither, stomp or fly in.

The puppets' feet must be on the ground when they are walking or standing. The illusion is quite lost if an elephant begins to float slowly upwards while talking. Children should also practise keeping puppets very still and moving only relevant parts of them – a lot of meaningless movement on a shadow screen is disastrous. Every movement should have a reason, or the puppet should remain still. Most important is the way the puppet walks. The children have to experiment and practise so that they fit the size of the footsteps to the size of the puppet and keep the feet in constant contact with the screen frame. Mention has already been made of weighting puppets' legs for ease of manipulation.

It is a general convention that whichever puppet is speaking should move, indicating that this is the one from whom the voice is coming, while others on screen are still, or react appropriately. This takes much practice, even in this relatively simple play. A good exercise to do before rehearsing the play is to make two characters stand opposite one another, perfectly still, then ask one of them to make a very small movement which affects the other – perhaps a slight tap. The other character should then react appropriately, and so on. Words can be added later. During rehearsals children become more and more subtle in their use of the puppets as their confidence and 'feel' for their figure grows, and it is a joy to watch when they have sequences well worked out.

I mentioned the use of several shadow screens, which can be very effective where you have a story which has distinct scenes. The play which ends this chapter, *A Father's Gifts*, is far more complex than *The Great Big Red Apple*, involving three brothers who journey in different directions with the presents their father has given them. This play would lend itself well to being done on three screens so that each brother's story could be told in a different place. The play is based on a Korean folk tale and although it is written with five narrators, these parts could be split if more speaking parts were needed.

A Father's Gifts
a shadow puppet play

Cast
Narrators 1-5
Old Father
Son 1 (with millstone)
Son 2 (with stick and gourd)
Son 3 (with drum)
Robber 1
Robber 2
Son 1's wife
Tokkaebi (a devil)
Wealthy Father
Wealthy Mother
'Dead' Daughter
Tiger
Villagers 1-4
Emperor
Emperor's wife
Emperor's daughter

Scene 1
Old Father's bedroom – he lies dying.

Narrator 1 Long, long ago in Korea there lived an old man who was very poor. He had three sons, and when he lay dying he summoned them to his bedside to say his last farewells to them and give them their inheritances.

Old Father (*To Son 1*) My eldest son – I have very little to leave you. Take this millstone – and who knows, one day it may bring you a great fortune. (*Hands him millstone*)

Son 1 Thank you father – I will take it with me wherever I go. Goodbye, dear father.

Old Father Goodbye, dear son. (*Son 1 exits; Son 2 enters*) My dear second-born son – farewell to you. I wish I had more to leave you, but all I have for your inheritance is this bamboo walking stick and this gourd bowl. Take them – and who knows, one day they may bring you a great fortune. (*Hands him walking stick and gourd bowl*)

Son 2 Thank you father – I will carry them with me wherever I go. Goodbye, dear father.

82

Old Father Goodbye, dear son. (*Son 2 exits; Son 3 enters*) Ah – my youngest son – farewell, my boy. My gift to you is very humble, I am afraid – but who knows, perhaps one day this drum will bring you a great fortune. (*Hands him drum*)

Son 3 Thank you father. It is not the richness of the gift which is important. I will never be without this drum – thank you. Goodbye, dear father.

Narrator 1 At that, the father died. Shortly after, the three sons set off to seek their fortunes – each carrying the gift he had received as his inheritance. They walked and walked until they came to a part of the road which split into three. Each took a different road and they said goodbye, promising to meet at the same spot ten years later.

Scene 2

Along the left-hand road.

Narrator 2   The eldest son chose the left-hand road and he trudged along with his millstone on his back till it was too dark to go any further. Then, afraid to sleep on the ground for fear of robbers and wild animals he climbed a tall tree, still carrying the millstone.

He was very tired indeed and soon fell asleep, but some time later he was wakened by the sound of voices. Two robbers had chosen to divide their treasure right beneath the tree he was sleeping in.

Robber 1   A diamond to me, a ruby to you; a sapphire to me, an emerald to you ...

Robber 2   Hey, wait a minute — that's not fair! Diamonds and sapphires are worth more than rubies and emeralds!

Robber 1   No they're not!

Robber 2   Yes they are!

Robber 1   They're NOT, they're NOT, they're NOT! NOT! NOT!

Narrator 2   Suddenly a dreadful noise from above stopped them in their tracks. (*Noise of thunder*)

Robber 2   Oh mercy me! It's a terrible wild animal — or a devil — or worse, right above our heads. Let's GO!

Narrator 2   And, leaving all their spoils, the two robbers ran away as fast as their legs would carry them. Then the eldest son stopped grinding his millstone, and climbing down from the tree he gathered up all the jewels and gold coins that were spread out on the ground.

It was almost morning, and he set off for the next village with his fortune, and before very long he had bought a large house and married a beautiful girl.

Son 1's wife Dearest – how lucky we both are! We have a wonderful house, beautiful furniture, a fragrant garden – and, best of all, we have each other.

Son 1 And all because of my father's inheritance – the millstone! It just goes to show – humble things can bring a fortune when wisely used!

Scene 3
Along the middle road.

Narrator 3 Meanwhile, the middle son had taken the middle road and it led him to a graveyard near a village. When darkness fell he settled down to sleep on a burial mound but was soon woken by the sound of heavy footsteps. A terrible voice called out to him.

Tokkaebi Come on, dead man – wake up and play with me!

Narrator 3 It was a tokkaebi – one of the devils who go about at night tormenting human souls. The middle son was not frightened, however.

Son 2 Of course – I would love to play!

Tokkaebi What's this? What's this? You do not sound DEAD!

Son 2 Certainly I am dead – feel my skull!

Narrator 3 And the middle son held out the gourd bowl for the tokkaebi to feel.

Tokkaebi Well ... yes ... your skull is certainly a dead man's skull. Let me feel your arm too.

Narrator 3 And so the middle son held out the bamboo walking stick for the tokkaebi to feel, and when he felt what he thought was a bone he was happy.

Tokkaebi Good! You certainly are a corpse – so you may come with me.

Son 2 Come where with you, may I ask?

Tokkaebi You will see, dead man – you will see!

Narrator 3 The tokkaebi led the middle son off into the night sky and at last they landed outside the home of a wealthy man. Then the devil told the son that he was going to steal the spirit of the daughter of the house, and he went inside. Soon he was back, carrying the spirit.

Tokkaebi   Here it is – look after it for me, dead man! I will see you tomorrow. (*Exits*)

Narrator 3   As soon as the tokkaebi had gone, the middle son went into the big house. Hearing sounds of crying, he realised that the daughter of the house had just died. He went to the girl's parents at once, still carrying her spirit in his hand.

Son 2   Excuse me for entering your house at a time like this – but I think I may be able to bring your daughter back to life.

Wealthy Father   But ... all the doctors in the land have told us there is nothing to be done ...

Wealthy Mother   Our daughter is sleeping her last sleep – she can never be woken.

Son 2   If you will allow me, I believe I can wake her.

Wealthy Father   Then please – she lies behind that door. Go in.

Son 2   There is one condition – I must be left alone with her.

Wealthy Father   We will not disturb you. (*Son 2 exits*)

Narrator 3   When the middle son was alone with the dead girl, he sealed up all the windows with rice paper and then he stood above the girl's body and carefully let her spirit leave his hand. With a noise like a

great wind blowing through a forest, the spirit flew round the girl's head and entered her body again, through her nostrils. Immediately, the girl woke and jumped up.

The middle son took her to her parents, who were overjoyed. Very soon the girl and boy were married at a great, rich wedding.

'Dead' Girl   Oh – how happy I am! You brought me back to life, and now we share our lives forever!

Son 2   And all because of my father's inheritance – the bamboo walking stick and the gourd bowl! It goes to show – humble things can bring a fortune when wisely used!

Scene 4
Along the right-hand road.

Narrator 4   While all this was going on, the youngest son had chosen to walk along the right-hand road, and as he walked he banged his drum. Suddenly he turned a corner and there, blocking his path and roaring ferociously, stood a huge tiger.

Tiger   ROOOOOAAAAAR!!

Son 3   Oh no! Oh dear me! What on earth shall I do?

Tiger   ROOOOOOOOOOOOAAAAAAAR!!!!

Son 3   (*Bangs his drum – the tiger stops roaring*) Aha! That's what it is – the tiger doesn't like me to stop banging my drum! Well, that is very simple then – as long as I bang, it will not eat me. So I will keep BANGING!!

Narrator 4   And so the youngest son walked on, banging his drum as loudly as he could, and the tiger danced along behind him, as happy and as friendly as a kitten. And when they reached the next village the people could not believe their eyes. They pointed at the man and his tame tiger, who danced in time to the drumbeat, and they even joined in themselves, singing and dancing with the rhythm.

Villager 1   Look! Look! A performing tiger! A tiger that can DANCE!

Villager 2   What a clever man that must be – taming a wild beast like that! (*Throws money*) Here, brave sir – have some of my gold. It is small payment for such a wonder!

Villager 3   And here's some more – for truly I have never seen a wonder like it.

Villager 4 I'll add to that – for such a brave and clever man deserves rich payment!

Narrator 4 Very soon the youngest son realised that he could easily make his fortune just by banging the drum, and so he led the tiger to the capital city. Before long the emperor himself heard about the boy and his performing tiger, and they were invited to the palace.

Emperor Wonderful! Wonderful! Second to none! Why – I think this young man should stay with us forever – don't you, my dear?

Emperor's wife Certainly he should – we shall be the envy of all the courts in the land with such a performer!

Emperor's daughter Oh good – for this man's bravery has melted my heart completely. Father – *dear* father – tell me I may marry him?

Narrator 4 The emperor agreed at once, and the two were married and lived a happy life together as prince and princess. The tiger lived in the palace too, and never showed any desire to be back in the wild.

Emperor's daughter What a wonderful life we have, beloved! And what a wonderful pet we have too!

Son 3 And all because of my father's inheritance – the drum! It goes to show – humble things can bring a fortune when wisely used!

Scene 5
Ten years later, at the place where the road splits.

Son 1 So here we all are again – back where we started all these years ago!

Son 2 And just look at us – each one richer than the next. Who would think we were the sons of a poor man?

Son 3 Not only have we made our fortunes and are rich, we are also as happy as we could possibly be – which is even more important!

Son 1 Well *I* must say, *I* would have none of this fortune if it had not been for *my* inheritance – the millstone!

Son 2 And *I* must say, *I* would have none of this fortune if it had not been for *my* inheritance – the bamboo walking stick and the gourd bowl!

Son 3 And *I* must say, *I* would have none of this fortune if it had not been for *my* inheritance – the drum!

Son 1 Yes, our father was right when he said we might all gain our fortunes from his humble gifts.

Son 2 It is as we have always said – humble things can bring a fortune when wisely used!

Song – *Our Father's Gifts*

All Sons   Our father's gifts weren't made of gold
They wouldn't be worth much if they were sold
But they brought us everything we were told
They brought us a fortune in happiness
They brought us a fortune in joy!

Son 1   A millstone isn't a joy to own
It's not made of silver or precious stone
But thanks to the millstone I'm not alone –
It's brought me a fortune in happiness
It's brought me a fortune in joy!

Son 2   A bamboo stick and an empty bowl
Are not made of riches to please the soul
But my father's presents have made me whole
They've brought me a fortune in happiness
They've brought me a fortune in joy!

Son 3   This drum of mine is a simple thing
It isn't a crown or a diamond ring
But when they hear it, the people sing –
It brings them a fortune in happiness
It brings them a fortune in joy!

**All Sons
+ Wives**   Some gifts are simple, some gifts are free
But if you add your ability
And use them wisely, then you will see –
They'll bring you a fortune in happiness
They'll bring you a fortune in joy!

Our Father's Gifts

Arranged by Marilyn Smellie

5

Projects

There is a fresco by Masaccio in the Brancacci Chapel in Florence, painted in 1427. Part of it is entitled *St Peter Healing the Sick with his Shadow.* In it St Peter is seen walking past a group of lame and blind people. He does not appear to stop or even look at them, but as his shadow falls on them they are miraculously cured.

This is another aspect of the magic of the shadow and although nowadays few people would take it literally, I have seen instances of the 'curative' function of the shadow in my work with shadow puppets. The shadow figure, as we have seen, is one step removed from the puppet itself – and if a puppet allows people to speak more easily through it, then perhaps the shadow of a puppet allows for even more security. Shadow theatre's quiet, lyrical quality has a calming effect – shadow puppets generally move slowly and their movements are seldom rough; they create an atmosphere of calm and allow you to rest within that calmness.

The kinds of projects I have undertaken in the past fall roughly into four categories: *Issue-based Shadow Puppetry, Lyrical Shadow Puppetry, Historical Shadow Puppetry* and *Scientific Shadow Puppetry.* There follow some examples under each heading, to show teachers the *kinds* of ways in which I use the medium. I hope they will be able to fit them to their own needs.

Issue-based Shadow Puppetry

Puppetry is used in the developing world to introduce issues and involve people in dealing with them. For example, in South Indian villages community organisations funded by Development Agencies such as OXFAM act out little puppet plays whose themes could concern caste, alcohol abuse, ownership of land, and so on. Such is the dearth of entertainment in rural areas that these 'animateurs' attract large audiences, and gradually an audience comes to realise that the issues are *their* issues – the puppets are *them*, or people relevant to them. At this point the animateurs leave to let discussion take place, and when they return with their puppets they can involve the people. And, speaking through their puppet characters, the villagers themselves can state their cases, express ideas that are important to them, act out possible solutions. They are thereby empowered to take up their own case, and to deal with issues in their own ways.

Shadow puppetry is a less direct medium so it is not used for this type of issue-based work. But it can still explore issues of all kinds and its 'hidden-ness' makes it particularly good when the issues are painful or embarrassing. Over the past four years I have been working with the Epilepsy Association of Scotland, usually with groups of people in their late teens who have epilepsy, or carers of people with the condition. For all our supposed 'enlightenment' there is still a surprising amount of ignorance about epilepsy, and sufferers often feel stigmatised. The ways in which we have used the shadow theatre could equally well be used to help people with other similarly misunderstood conditions to express their feelings.

One good way to get people talking about a sensitive subject is to ask them to devise a shadow presentation for a younger audience. This gives them a focus for their discussions and it also makes them think about how best to explain clearly why they feel the way they do. So they become less self-conscious, perhaps because they are more concerned with their potential audience than with their peers.

Stories using animal characters can make discussing serious problems easier – and humour, well placed, can be a godsend. I have a story about a little mouse called Eric who develops epilepsy when he is chased by Sinbad, the tiger-like cat who appears one day to shatter the peace of Eric's idyllic, cheese-filled home. It is a scientific fact that many small mammals exhibit seizures in life-threatening situations, and so epilepsy can be seen as a defence mechanism. After hearing Eric's adventure, groups set about writing similar stories using their own favourite animals and then make these characters into shadow puppets and perform the stories on the shadow screen.

There could, for example, be a play about a little rabbit who has a seizure in class. First the teacher notices that his attention is wandering, and she tells him to wake up. Then he falls down and begins to twitch, and the teacher (who knows exactly what to do) tells everyone else to keep calm and move the chairs out of his way. She puts him into the coma position and, while they wait for him to come round, the rest of the class gets on with their work. Or the story could demonstrate how *not* to treat someone with epilepsy, with perhaps another animal character telling the audience what Bertie Badger *should* have done! Thus have countless problems been explored in as light-hearted and candid a way as possible – and much has been learned. In a similar way, an upper primary class could discuss how best to treat someone with asthma, diabetes, or some other condition which makes a child feel 'different'.

Bullying is an ever-present problem in schools, and racist bullying can go on even in schools where the overall ethos is positive. Shadow theatre could bring problems out into the open – and if a young audience is targeted and animal characters used there will be no problems of confidentiality because no names are named. Racism can be effectively explored through puppets from other planets. What do little Red men from Planet Krypton think of the little Blue men who also live there? They have different ways of doing things – but are they 'wrong'? Or could the two different 'cultures' perhaps find that together they have a Purple culture which is even richer than either of the original ones?

Sexism too can be explored using animal 'models'; indeed, all kinds of stereotypes can be broken down if you begin to create cowardly lions who can cry, and brave mice who face what they most fear, and female animals who are just as daring as their male counterparts.

Bereavement can also be handled on the shadow screen in a way which would otherwise be difficult to do. I was recently privileged to work with a class of nine year olds who had just lost a classmate to cystic fibrosis. Their teacher wanted them to present a tribute to their friend, but it would have been difficult for each child to express their feelings for her 'cold' on a stage in front of the whole school and the girl's parents. The children first wrote short poems to say what she had meant to them. *Haiku* can be good for work of this kind because they are very short, do not need to rhyme, and have a tight structure which helps focus ideas and get rid of unnecessary words. An example of a Japanese *haiku* is:

> *Butterfly, sleep well*
> *Bright spot on the temple bell*
> *Until it rings – ding!*

The poem derives its structure from its syllable pattern, which is 5:7:5. *Haiku* are usually used to describe aspects of nature.

After writing the poems the children had to find images which 'matched' the sentiments in them. This is a challenging thing to do and is an art we should be encouraging from very early on. One simple image worked particularly well – a child made the outline of a heart from black card and filled it with different shades of pink and red tissue paper. Then she cut it in two and put each half onto a rod. Her poem spoke of how her heart had felt as though it was broken and would never heal when her friend had died, but how as time passed she felt the sad memories being replaced by happy ones. As she described her broken heart mending, the two halves were slowly brought together and held for a moment on the screen.

Other poems simply recalled things the girl had liked to do, like riding her pony, sailing in ships, and listening to her favourite pop group. Each child was able to perform his/her poem without breaking down, and it was only afterwards that the tears flowed. The girl's mother came up to me afterwards and said, 'I didn't know she could dance', referring to a small detail in the poem of one of the boys. This personal touch was immensely moving – and the incident beautifully parallels the philosophy behind the *wayang kulit*, the shadow puppets which enable the dead to live on.

All kinds of more mundane issues can be expressed through shadow puppetry. I have made enormous cigarettes with red cellophane tips to proclaim how bad smoking is for health; endangered animals can give their own message about caring for the environment; shadow policemen can stop a young jaywalker and explain the Green Cross Code, and so on. Most class projects have some area which can be enlivened by shadow puppetry, and a short stint of shadow theatre done in this way can give a boost to a topic which is losing its momentum.

Extracts from novels can be dramatised in shadow theatre. Take the account of the escape of slaves to Canada, *Underground to Canada* by Barbara Smucker. Many parts of the book lend themselves to dramatisation – we wrote poems as if we were one of the slave characters, then made our characters and their friends as shadow figures.

The final project in this category concerns the issue of 'homelessness'. Again we began by writing short poems about homelessness, after discussing at some length what 'home' means to us and what we would most miss if we had no home. Then shadow puppets were made, the emphasis being on simplicity. (A good way to get this point over is to show children signs, like road signs and logos, which owe their clarity to their lack of detail, in the capturing of the meaningful line.) One poem spoke of the city at night, and a few stars sparkled on the screen while soft, haunting music played and a blue filter covered the light source. Then a lone figure appeared, walked slowly across the screen and lay down under the stars. With very little in the way of words, an atmosphere was created which was memorable.

Lyrical Shadow Puppetry

Many of the examples described under *Issue-based Shadow Puppetry* would also fit into this category. It is the way I think shadow puppetry is best used: to interpret poems, songs and music.

Published poems which adapt well to the shadow screen are hard to find, and I prefer to use children's own material. Long, ballad-style poems can work well as long as they have sufficient characters, but the published poetry I've found most successful has been that of our Bard, Robert Burns. A poem like the well-known *Tam O' Shanter* – which we Scots recite in full when we celebrate Burns' Suppers – could be rather long-winded if performed in full. But someone can recite a lengthy poem while short scenes from it are performed on screen.

Or the poems could serve as a starting point for the discussion and the fleshing-out of characters. We know Tam's wife was a 'sulky, sullen dame' who sat waiting for him to come back from the pub, 'Gathering her brows like gathering storm/Nursing her wrath to keep it warm', but what did she actually *say* to her friend as they sat together tapping their feet in frustration? And what, in the meantime, were Tam's friends saying to persuade him not to go home till later? And while everyone knows that Tam watched the witches dance round Alloway Kirk, *how* did they dance? And to what tune? Are there modern pop songs which would lend themselves to a witches' dance? This opens up discussion of the idea of the witch as 'wise woman' – another example of myth-dispelling. The shadow figures the children made in response were mainly created out of the plants that grew round their country school, with the odd feather stuck on as clothes or hair.

Burns' poems are so full of wonderfully descriptive Scots words that a performance cannot fail to be lively. Particularly in areas of South West Scotland where a dialect of Scots is still the first language of most children, we are aware of maintaining our Scots tongue, and puppetry is an excellent medium. Minority languages or dialects in parts of England, Ireland, and Wales have similarly expressive words and idioms that it would be sad to lose.

Certain of Burns' short poems are particularly successful and here is one which looks really good in performance. As any Scottish farmer's child will tell you, a 'Hoggie' is a young sheep which has not yet lost her virginity!

My Hoggie

What will I do gin my Hoggie die?
My joy, my pride, my Hoggie!
My only beast, I had nae mae,
And vow but I was vogie!
The lee-lang night we watch'd the fauld,
Me and my faithfu' doggie;
We heard nocht but the roaring linn,
Amang the braes sae scroggie.

But the houlet cry'd frae the castle wa',
The blitter frae the boggie;
The tod reply'd upon the hill,
I trembled for my Hoggie.
When day did daw, and cocks did craw,
The morning it was foggie;
An unco tyke, lap o'er the dyke,
And maist has kill'd my Hoggie!

vogie: well-pleased, vain; *linn*: a waterfall; *scroggie*: thickly grown with stunted shrubs; *houlet*: owl; *blitter*: mire snipe; *tod*: fox.

After discussing the poem's meaning and its unfamiliar words, children made either a shepherd or one of the predators. There was a blue filter for the 'lee-lang night' and a red filter for the day 'dawing', and a background was created by drawing a 'dyke' onto overhead projector acetate and sticking pieces of dry grass and heathers around it to create a pastoral scene. Because the poem is so short, it was performed a number of times so that each group could show their work, and far from being tedious, it was intriguing to see the different interpretations. After the performances the children knew the poem well, and were easily persuaded to write their own verses: which other animals might the shepherd hear – perhaps one which did not make him fear for his sheep's safety?

Alternatively, you can start with the puppets. Let children make any character they fancy and then play the character on the screen to build up a picture of its special characteristics: how it moves, the way it speaks, what it eats if it is an animal, and so on. This can be a great stimulus for poetry writing. In a similar way, after discussing and making some of the Karagöz characters, ten year olds wrote a class acrostic using Hacivat's name:

H acivat is very kind
A nd he likes to use his mind
C aring for people is his way
I n Bursa town he holds great sway
V ery good at money sums
A nd Karagöz and he are chums
T he Turkish theatre's where they play.

Then each child had a go. Jeremiah decided to write in his first language:

H acivat est amusant
A vec son copain Karagöz
C omme il est bon à des multiplications!
I l est fait de peau de chameau
V enant de Bursa en Turkey
A la rue, il fait rigoles tous le monde
T ous les gents s'arrètent pour l'écouter.

The role of music in shadow theatre has already been indicated: *Carnival of the Animals* and *Peter and the Wolf* would be obvious choices. Song can be used in the same way as poetry.

Historical Shadow Puppetry

The Turkish Shadow Theatre described in the first chapter fits this category of shadow puppetry, which is a lively and interactive way of bringing the past alive or communicating information about museum exhibits and the like.

When children are taken to a museum or Art Gallery and sketch one of the exhibits, they become personally involved with whatever statue, or character from a picture, or stuffed animal they choose to draw. If they then make shadow figures from the sketches and copy down the written information about the exhibit and turn it into a little script, the drawings will have new life. Although the children may look with interest at the drawings of their classmates, presenting these drawings on the shadow screen enables everyone to enjoy and share each exhibit and the information about it. The shadow production can also be shown to other classes.

A group of rather dull Victorian carvings gained a new lease of life with this treatment, and we were lucky to find a poem written shortly after the statues were made which told the story of each character in a way which was very much in keeping with the figures themselves. The class brought the story up to date by writing a short play about a group of modern-day children who visit the statues and are left wondering who are really the ghosts – they or the statues.

Wall carvings in stately homes can be similarly used, and the inevitable family portraits give excellent detail of clothes and hairstyles so that the original owners can be fitted out to come back and haunt National Trust visitors. A shadow puppetry workshop in an Adam-designed hunting lodge was based on Adam's plasterwork, which featured hunting motifs, and the final presentation became a debate about whether or not hunting was justified. It is the one anti-hunting debate where the fox himself makes an appearance – and puts a very good case for banning it.

Social history too lends itself to shadow theatre. There is an area in Glasgow called Castlemilk, where families were rehoused in the '50s from poor accommodation in places like Govan. Such were the numbers shifted that it was called the 'Big Flit'. The reactions of the residents to their 'luxurious' new flats has been well documented by the local History group, which recorded these people describing their feelings and experiences. Young people were astounded to hear how 'countrified' the area had been, the delight of the new occupants with their inside toilets, and so on. When they each made a shadow figure of one of the incomers they spoke their words again – much to the interest and amusement of their local audience.

This is a category of shadow theatre where overhead projector transparencies can be particularly effective. Supposing your school is near a site of historical interest, a castle, perhaps – take the children out and photograph the key sites, then photocopy the resulting photographs on to OHP film. Projecting the scenes onto a screen creates an instant backdrop for shadow perfor-mances. Slides can also be used for this, projecting the images through a slide projector, but the light tends to be too dazzling with normal screens and the projector fan rather noisy.

Paintings can be similarly explored, limited only by resources and imagina-tion. A detail from a painting by Breughel, for instance, full of lively characters and action, could be projected and discussed. Ask the children who the characters are, where they are and what they are doing, then have each child choose a character and make it – possibly as a translucent shadow puppet, imitating the colours as closely as possible. The puppets are placed on the screen on top of their frozen counterparts, and at a given signal the OHP transparency is taken away and we hear what is on the characters' minds. Abstract pictures can also provide splendid backdrops. One of Mondrian's, for example could be projected and used as a kind of abstract environment. What is happening in the red square? The blue? With imaginative music, what an exciting *son et lumière* ensues. And no child involved will ever forget the content of that picture. The example of Mondrian leads into the final category:

Scientific Shadow Puppetry

This is the rather off-putting term I give shadow theatre when it is used to communicate scientific facts or principles. A few examples will show that it is in fact extremely user-friendly.

Shadow theatre demonstrates colour mixing extremely well. I use it with very young children, as described in Chapter 7, to practise colour recognition and then show how secondary colours are formed from the primary ones. Better still is to have older children designing performances for the little ones.

A class of nine year olds who were studying Light as part of a Science project were asked to work in groups to produce a simple story for teaching the principle of colour mixing to the youngest class. The importance of simplicity of language, repetition, audience participation and humour were discussed, as well as the need for good clear figures. The class came up with a host of imaginative ideas. They had a yellow surfer whose face turned a lovely shade of green when a blue wave covered him; there were three little kittens, Red, Blue and Yellow, whose mother couldn't understand why when they played together their colours mysteriously altered; and there were pop singers in different coloured costumes who sang about their colour changes. Such performances could be scripted and put together by, say, a glove puppet 'Colour Wizard'.

The photograph overleaf shows an example of 'scientific' shadow puppetry taken from a story called *The Dragons' Colour Magic* (*Word Play*, 1997). Two dragons, Redtum and Yellowtum, live in a land which is made up of only these two colours. They are quite happy until a magic ball of every colour appears. The dragons set off to find all these colours, which they do by landing in differently coloured environments which change the colour of their tummies. This is the kind of example to offer older children devising colour mixing stories.

Children who have experienced the colour mixing of *light* may find these shows confusing. The phenomenon of mixing lights (*additive colour mixing*) is not the same as the mixing of paints or coloured cellophane, which is *subtractive colour mixing*. So there is a different system of primary and secondary colours: for example, red mixed with green produces yellow. Obviously this is a complex subject and one best explained in Primary Science books.

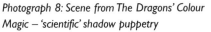
Photograph 8: Scene from The Dragons' Colour Magic – 'scientific' shadow puppetry

Phenomena like the Water Cycle can be demonstrated on the shadow screen, moving clouds until they come to rest over a mountain top and change into raindrops. The presentation can be enlivened in numerous ways: by making flowers or trees grow, or showing the fish at the bottom of a river.

Shadow puppetry can illustrate life cycles vividly. You can make effective tadpoles by cutting out the body with a thin 'tail' and sticking it on to a much fatter 'tail' cut out of tracing paper. The spawn can also be made like this: a black card circle stuck on to a bigger tracing paper circle makes a convincing jelly-covered egg. Frogs are rather more difficult (see photograph bottom left).

Caterpillars are a hugely popular shadow form. They can be simply made out of seven or eight black card circles – the first and last with a nose and tail respectively – given a pattern using a hole punch or needle and backed with several different colours, then all joined together with split pins. Against a background of flowers or leaves, real or drawn, the caterpillars can be shown as the 'eating machines' they are. If one or two tall grass stalks are included, then when they have eaten their fill they can climb high and wave their heads around as they pupate, rolling themselves up to show this stage. At the appropriate

Photograph 9: Frog and tadpole puppets – The Magic of Spring

moment (timing is of the essence here) the 'cocoons' are whisked off and butterflies brought into view, flapping nearer and nearer the screen until they alight on the vegetation and show off the symmetrical patterns on their wings.

In Chapter 3 the importance of 'necks' was stressed, and the same applies to butterflies. It is important to provide a little 'joint' piece when making the wings, otherwise the butterfly will not fly well because too much of its wings will overlap the body section. To make butterflies symmetrical – and they make good items for practising maths – cut out one wing then draw round it for the second. And do make that body section nice and *fat* – slim elegant butterflies have a short shelf-life.

This chapter ends with *The Magic of the Spring*, written to show three life cycles. It also has a puppet 'magician' who could be a sock puppet or a rod or glove puppet. I have called him Willie the Wizard but he could equally well be an animal character. The play is intended, like so much of this book, as a starting point for your own ideas – you might read it to a class and let them write their own versions. The song can be set to your own tune or one invented by the children or it can be recited and more verses can be added.

The Magic of the Spring

Willie   (*appearing suddenly*) Hello boys and girls! My name's Willie the Wizard. Can you say 'hello' to me?

Audience Hello Willie!

Willie   Oh dear me, I can't hear you. Hello boys and girls!

Audience (*slightly louder*) Hello Willie!

Willie   I still can't hear you – you'll have to shout. Hello boys and girls!

Audience (*very loud*) HELLO WILLIE!!!

Willie   (*rubbing his ears*) That's better – I heard that. Now – do you like magic, boys and girls?

Audience Oh yes!

Willie   Good – because I've got some *pretty impressive* magic to show you today
and   – and I've brought my magic screen to show it on. But you know, boys
              girls, the kind of magic that I'm going to show you today isn't any old
              magic. It's very very *special* magic. In fact, it's called *Spring Magic*. So – you
              just look at the magic screen and you'll see ...

FROG MAGIC

Lights dim and screen lights come on with blue filter. As the song is sung or spoken, frog spawn floats about, then is replaced by tadpoles, and finally frogs.

Here's some frog spawn slippy and wet
With a little black dot inside ...
It looks like jelly that's hardly set
With a little black dot inside!

But just you look – they've all got tails
And the little black dot's a head ....
And now they look like tiny whales
And the little black dot's a head!

Remove blue filter; insert 'log' background

Now see what's hopping along the logs
And that little black dot has GONE ...
The tadpoles have changed into frogs
And they'll lay their own frog spawn!

Did you ever see such a thing before?
It's a really magic thing!
Yet it's all around for us all to see ...
That's the magic of the spring!

102

*Screen lights out; lights on **Willie** who appears again*

Willie   Wasn't that good? Imagine a piece of wobbly jelly turning into a *frog* – that's the magic of the spring! Now, watch for the next piece of magic – ready? This time it's ...

FLOWER MAGIC

Lights dim and screen lights come on. Bulbs appear at the bottom of the screen and as the song is sung/spoken they are replaced by bulbs with tall green shoots and finally by daffodils and tulips.

Here are some bulbs all sleeping tight
In their cosy bed of soil
Through the long cold winter's night
In their cosy bed of soil

Then a long green stem shoots up so high
And it grows to feel the sun ...
It's reaching up towards the sky
As it grows to feel the sun

Now see what's in the flower bed –
As the sun is shining down
There's lots of flowers, yellow and red
And the sun is shining down!

Did you ever see such a thing before?
It's a really magic thing!
Yet it's all around for us all to see ...
That's the magic of the spring!

Screen lights out; lights on Willie who appears again

Willie   Now, wasn't that amazing? Who would have thought you could get big tall flowers like that from just a tiny little brown bulb. That's the magic of the spring for you! Do you want to see another piece of spring magic, boys and girls?

Audience Yes please.

Willie   Can't hear you! Do you want to see another piece of spring magic, boys and girls?

Audience (*much louder*) YES PLEASE!!!

Willie   (*rubbing ears again*) OK, OK, no need to burst a fellow's eardrums! Watch the screen now – this time it's ...

BUTTERFLY MAGIC

Lights dim and screen lights come on. The daffodils and tulips remain on the screen and as the second verse of the song is sung/spoken caterpillars appear and crawl slowly to the tops of the flowers where they change into butterflies.

Here's a magic you can't see at all
You would have to come so close!
For they're stuck to the leaves and they're very small
You would have to come so close!

Red filter

But look what happens when the sun is high
And the tiny eggs have hatched ...
The caterpillars come crawling by
For the tiny eggs have hatched

Remove red filter; remove caterpillars and flowers

And in summertime look in the sky
And a lovely sight you'll see ...
Each one is now a butterfly –
What a lovely sight to see!

Did you ever see such a thing before?
It's a really magic thing!
Yet it's all around for us all to see ...
That's the magic of the spring!

Screen lights out; lights on Willie who appears again

Willie So, boys and girls, there it is – the magic of the spring! It changes eggs into tadpoles so that in the summer there are frogs, and it makes the first green shoots appear so that flowers can grow, and it starts all the changes that make butterflies appear. I think it's a very good magic – do you?

Audience Yes!

Willie Let's have one last look at all the things that come from spring magic ...

Frogs, flowers and butterflies appear and float round the screen

When we first began, while the earth still slept,
We were each a different thing -
Then the sun shone down and the earth awoke ...
That's the magic of the spring!

6

The curriculum

In junior schools today it is rarely possible for busy teachers to do something 'just for fun' – the demands of the curriculum are always to be met, and sometimes it seems that every waking minute must be recorded in terms of the Key Skill it teaches and the Range it covers. So, although I have referred to the curriculum in general terms throughout the book, this chapter specifies some of the ways Language work arising out of shadow puppetry fits into the *English in the National Curriculum* (England) and the *English Language 5-14* (Scotland) guidelines. These two documents say much the same things about the teaching of Language. I propose, therefore, to discuss Language teaching through shadow puppetry in relation to both.

Four different aspects of Language are identified. In Scotland these are referred to as 'outcomes' and described as 'Listening' (which can also include 'Watching' – a very important point for our purposes), 'Talking', 'Reading' and 'Writing'. In England the two first categories are described together as 'Speaking and Listening'.

The Scottish guidelines lay particular emphasis on the 'purposes' of Language, and the following extract supports the case for shadow puppetry:

> A sense of purpose and audience gives speakers and writers greater control over their language and its effects. Grasping the purposes behind a piece of talk or writing helps listeners and readers make better sense of its meaning and assists them in measuring its success. Furthermore, the contexts in which language is expressed and received have a profound influence on any communication and comprehension.

'Purpose' and 'Audience' are two things which shadow puppetry projects serve well. Even if yours is not a full-scale *Puppet Company* topic with a Grand Tour planned to the local Nursery, the knowledge that they are working towards a 'performance' gives children a great sense of purpose. It is a treat to be asked to read a story to the little ones – how much more of a thrill to show off *all* your talents in one fell swoop. And that sense of purpose lies not only in the prospect of the show but gives a lift to all the related writing tasks, as described in Chapter 2. There is nothing like a real-life situation to banish the drudgery of letter- or instruction-writing.

As for 'Audience', a good sense of audience is worth a dozen Thesauruses and it is the essence of shadow puppetry work. The 'context', particularly where a Puppet Company is set up, is so real, and contains so many different aspects, that the potential Language tasks within it are limitless.

To demonstrate how shadow puppetry fits into English Language curricular requirements, there follows an indication of how some of the 'Purposes' listed under the Scottish 'outcomes' can be served by a *Puppet Company* topic, plus the relevant points from the English guidelines. Although the Scottish guidelines separate out Listening and Talking, these will be dealt with together for convenience. Where the purpose described for *Talking*, differs from that described for *Listening*, this is noted in brackets.

Listening and Talking

... to obtain information and respond appropriately (to convey information): Combined with the equally important 'Watching', this purpose is fulfilled when, for example, a willing puppeteer shows the class how s/he deals with problems of transportation etc., how s/he makes and uses puppets, how s/he chooses suitable material – and so on. It is also met, perhaps even more usefully, when Ranjit stands up in front of the class to give his illustrated talk on how he designed his Patent Shadow Puppet Holder. And it gives an extra dimension when a class is listening to a potential story for dramatisation – not only are they enjoying the story for itself, they are also picturing it transformed into another medium and judging its effectiveness. This goal also makes children focus on illustrations, which as they get older become less dominant in the books they are 'supposed' to be reading. It is good to have an excuse to sit down with a top junior (Primary Seven) class and enjoy a good picture book written for 5 year olds – no one needs to feel they are being patronised, and it allows the slow readers to join in.

... to establish relationships and interact with others: You soon find out who your friends are when you are squashed up against them in the dark under an uncomfortably warm anglepoise lamp and you have forgotten your cue! All types of drama rely on relating and interacting with other performers as well as with the all-important audience, and shadow theatre is a fine way of training children to listen in order to interact.

... to appreciate the feelings of others (to express feelings): This purpose of listening and watching is fulfilled in various ways in shadow theatre work. When children are at the stage where they have already made their puppet, they may welcome a short improvisation time to build the puppet's character. This is a time for everyone to listen to responses to questions in order to determine the character of the puppet, so that later they can write an appropriate part for it in their story. Not surprisingly, feelings voiced by the puppet are often strongly rooted in the problems of its maker, and these can be safely expressed and responded to. A playground argument can look remarkably trivial when it is presented on the screen, and the puppets allow different responses to be explored and candidly analysed.

Shadow theatre work can help boost confidence and develop the skills to express feelings by developing methods of positive criticism. As a teacher you may want children to learn how to criticise – there are ways to tell your classmate that his sea-horse looks more like a spiny ant-eater, and perhaps needs its nose cropped! And when children design and make a character and act with it on the screen, they lay themselves wide open. It is extremely important that children learn to develop the appropriate language. I have seen a puppet-making session develop into a Personal and Social Development class when someone is accused of rudeness and insensitivity about another's work. Skills can be safely learned here which can have a lasting effect on other behaviour.

... to reflect upon ideas, experiences and opinions (to present, share, clarify and reflect on ideas, experiences and opinions): Reflecting on others' ideas happens whenever a new puppet is made, a new screen design is produced, a new storyline suggested. 'Miss – she's copying me!', is a familiar wail. But in the continual sharing of ideas and new-found skills that goes on in puppetry work, 'copying' a good idea is soon acknowledged as a process that leads on to 'adaptation' and often to improvement. Experiences too are continually shared – the child who spoils her shadow figure by punching the joint hole too near the edge shares the frustration, shows the result, and others take care not to make the same mistake. Enacting situations and suggesting possible ways of resolving them through puppetry also fulfils this purpose of Language, for it enables a clarification and reflection on ideas and experiences.

... to gain imaginative and aesthetic pleasure (to give imaginative and aesthetic pleasure): Listening to and watching the results of long weeks of preparation is the culmination of puppetry work, and it undoubtedly gives aesthetic pleasure and stimulates imagination. The flow of imaginative ideas that arise from watching a shadow play often needs to be stemmed – for even

well into rehearsals children can always see *another* possibility, *another* sound effect you could add, *another* great line a character could say or way it could move. It is part of the discipline of drama to accept the point at which the performance is 'fixed', beyond which no further additions and alterations can be made – but still the little wheels of imagination whirr on in the darkness!

From the 'Speaking and Listening' category in the English document the following list, taken from Key Stages 1 and 2, consists of statements which relate to puppetry work in similar ways to those just described:

> *... Pupils should be given opportunities to talk for a range of purposes, including: telling stories, both real and imagined; imaginative play and drama; reading and listening to nursery rhymes and poetry, learning some by heart; exploring, developing and clarifying ideas; predicting outcomes and discussing possibilities; describing events, observations and experiences; making simple, clear explanations of choices; giving reasons for opinions and choices; reading aloud, telling and enacting stories and poems; presenting to audiences, live or on tape.*

Of particular interest is the notion of 'learning by heart'. Perhaps regarded as a little 'old-fashioned', it is a good way to give children the feel for rhythm in writing, teaching them the melody of prose. Learning by heart is usually reserved for poetry, but to learn lines of narrative has its own value, for good patterns of descriptive writing are thus internalised and will emerge later in the children's own work.

Taped soundtracks are rather dodgy, and although some professional puppeteers use them, most would not. They tend to sound rather cold and remote, and if anything untoward happens it can be a disaster because the soundtrack keeps playing while the action stops. But they can be quite effective in certain situations, and they provide an enjoyable way of practising Language skills. For example, if a small group of children find a play in their reading book that they could present to the rest of the class with shadow puppets but haven't time to make it into a big production, they could put the script on tape at their own speed, then use their tape to practise with their puppets. The result won't be brilliant but it will be 'all their own work' – and the great advantage of taping children's voices is that as they listen to themselves they notice difficulties they are having, perhaps with pronunciation, and begin to correct themselves. Better still is to let children record the whole performance on video if you have one. This is the only way the puppeteers can see their own work and assess the whole show.

At Key Stage 2, the English document says:

> ... *pupils should be given opportunities to communicate to different audiences and to reflect on how speakers adapt their vocabulary, tone, pace and style.*

It is through such reflection that the true art of the storyteller is learned – understanding the needs of listeners, interacting with them, repeating an important point, explaining anything the audience may find difficult to understand; in other words, getting inside the skin not only of the characters, but of the audience. The document goes on :

> ... *pupils should be given opportunities to participate in a wide range of drama activities, including improvisation, role-play, and the writing and performance of scripted drama. In responding to drama, they should be encouraged to evaluate their own and others' contribution.*

What better justification for a teacher to spend a month with a Language group dramatising a story or poem in their reading book? Or even to leave the reading book aside for a while to work on the children's own ideas which may arise from it?

Finally, under the 'Standard English and Language Study' section:

> ...*the range of pupils' vocabulary should be extended and enriched through activities that focus on words and their meanings, including language used in drama, role-play and word games.*

Reading scripts to children for them to use as models for their own writing will familiarise them with terms such as 'character', 'cast', 'scene', 'act', 'props', 'scenery', 'narrator'. Stage directions are an excellent way of introducing and practising adverbs – characters delivering their lines 'quietly', 'angrily', 'furiously', and so on. And for a fine example of word play, see Chapter 1 and Karagöz, with his dreadful puns!

Reading
... to obtain information and respond appropriately:

When doing the *Puppet Company* topic, certain reference materials are useful to have in the classroom. For example, shadow puppetry invites study of the geography of the East, so there would be a world map on the wall. As each shadow puppetry culture is introduced its place of origin can be located, and as time goes on and the children's knowledge grows, the routes by which shadow theatre is supposed to have spread can be traced – from Indonesia to

Turkey, from China to France. It intrigues children that no one is sure where and when the art arose or exactly how it spread, and to discuss the evidence for the theories. History has been inaccurately presented in school textbooks of the past (see Klein, 1985) and it is important that children do not blindly accept that what they read is necessarily correct.

One relevant 'strand' of 'Reading' is *'reading to reflect on the writers' ideas and craft'*. When adapting a story for the shadow screen, it has to be decided whether to have a narrator. As shown in my examples, a series of narrators works well. Writing the narrators' parts teaches a great deal about the craft of writing: how the writer sets a scene, introduces characters, moves the plot along, and achieves a good ending.

'Awareness of genre' has an important place in both sets of guidelines, and this too is fostered when material is being considered for the shadow screen. The questions that arise are: what kind of story is it? Is it fiction or non-fiction? Is it a myth? If so, is it a creation myth? If it is a poem, is it a narrative poem or is it more lyrical? This kind of in-depth look at literature encourages children to see whose 'voice' predominates in a story. *Who* is the narrator? Is it one of the characters – telling the story as it happens or looking back? Should the narration be in standard English or a dialect or in the archaic language of the court jester?

Under 'Reading' in the English guidelines the importance is noted of *'shared reading of play scripts'*, and *'the use of language that benefits from being read aloud and reread'*, with particular mention of *'myths, legends, and traditional stories'*. And under the 'Standard English and Language Study' section it is recommended that terms such as *'setting, plot and format'* be introduced.

Writing

'Functional' and 'imaginative' writing are two 'strands' listed in the Scottish guidelines. *Functional writing* lends itself to writing instructions on how to make puppets or build screens and preparing reports. 'Technology' and 'Mathematics' also depend heavily on Language. Where the Design Process is being stressed and children are having to test and adapt and re-test – as in a *Puppet Company* topic – appropriate vocabulary and writing style must be learned. Children soon learn the importance of accuracy in descriptions of processes and methods if their instructions are read aloud and then followed to the letter. The results can be bizarre and highlight the need for clarity in functional writing. Writing abridged versions of plays for inclusion in pro-grammes is a challenging aspect of functional writing. Good précis writing requires being able to extract the salient points of the piece – and the process of dramatisation with its splitting into scenes and use of narrator is good preparation.

Functional letter-writing can be made easier if children are clear about what information they want to impart. Posters announcing the place and time of a puppet play also provide the information to put in a letter to potential school audiences. And if experience has shown you that people sitting too far out to the side of the screen can't see, and someone has complained because the extension for the lights doesn't stretch far enough, the requirements in terms of space and equipment will be set out clearly in the letter.

Imaginative writing: The process of character building is a good way into writing imaginative stories. Children's imagination too often runs away with them: plots become far too complicated, characters are brought in willy-nilly without introduction, and the main thread can become hopelessly lost in a fankle of sub-plots. But when the purpose of imaginative writing is a good story for a play, the teacher can help the children bring the story under control. 'Don't you think there would be too many characters on at once?' tells your aspiring dramatists to simplify the plot; and constant reference to the comprehension of a younger audience will focus children down, teach them to discard irrelevancies which only confuse, and concentrate on the main point of the story. It is also a useful excercise for children to adapt a story they know which has a clever plot, a good style, and a clear structure.

The English guidelines on 'Writing' give significant weight to drama:

> *Pupils should be given opportunities to write in response to a variety of stimuli, including stories, plays and poems ... Pupils should be taught to identify the purpose for which they write and to write for a range of readers ... They should be taught to write in a range of forms, incorporating some of the different characteristics of those forms ... eg stories, poems, dialogues, drama scripts, invitations, instructions. They should be taught to use features of layout and presentation.*

The importance of layout and presentation is particularly demonstrated in shadow theatre work. If a child writes a script and fails to separate the characters' names from their speeches, the 'actors' will complain that the script is hard to follow. Children might well find teachers pedantic in their insistence on capital letters, full stops and paragraphs, but these conventions were not invented to torment pupils but to make meaning clearer and reading easier. Because their scripts will be used, children are given an object lesson in the need for clear layout. These skills can be practised on the word processor: 'bold' character names stand out, stage directions can be put in italics, and so on.

Puppetry can be used effectively in other curricular areas: Environmental Studies areas such as Technology, Geography and History can be brought alive; in Mathematics shape, symmetry, money (how much will we actually *make* if we charge 20p a ticket?), area (how many seats can we fit into our performance space?), measurement, and so on. Personal and Social Development crops up repeatedly, particularly in issue-based work; and Religious and Moral Education can have a puppetry input to teach a Bible story, celebrate a festival or explore what the history of shadow theatre teaches us about a particular religion. Expressive Arts will offer many opportunities to extend a project into sound and movement on the shadow screen, possibly in conjunction with music, dance or other forms of drama, where a certain part of a play may be presented on a shadow screen such as a dream sequence or time travel.

A final quote from English in the National Curriculum shows how shadow theatre could be used at Key Stages 3 and 4 to analyse and practise complex and difficult literary techniques:

> ... *the portrayal of setting and period, the weaving of parallel narratives, time shifts, the building of suspense, the use of imagery.*

All these points can be greatly enhanced by visual interpretation. Using shadow theatre to develop ideas can interweave language and imagery, reality and fantasy, past and present and, because the effects of shadow theatre are limited only by the imagination, the future.

7

The early years

Very young children learn through play. Nurseries and reception classes generally have puppets: a little furry character to help read the children stories and comment on them works so well because the children quickly engage with it and their imaginations bring it to life. But what about shadow puppetry in the early years? Its very attributes of lending distance and allowing the operator to remain hidden surely limit its suitability for very young children? As a medium for role play and character building this is true – far better to make paper plate or sock puppets which can interact with each other and their makers.

But this is not to say that shadow theatre does not have a place in the nursery. Educating young children is all about exposing them to different experiences and stimuli, and experimenting with colour, light and shape fascinates pre-school children. I use the shadow screen more and more at pre-school level, and have found Nursery teachers eager to use it with their classes for story-telling and to accompany songs and rhymes.

Teachers can make simple figures, perhaps incorporating a colour or a number into their design, and the children can learn how to make them appear on the screen with large dowel rods, as described in Chapter 3. Counting songs like the one about 'five little firemen' who disappear one by one to fight the fire until none is left are ideal to enact on the screen, and if each fireman wears a different number the 'performance' can be used to reinforce counting. Children have to listen attentively to the words of the song if they are to move at the right time, so cooperation and awareness of others is enhanced.

Similarly with Nursery rhymes: *Hickory Dickory Dock* can show a little sequence where the shadow mouse runs up and down the clock, *Humpty Dumpty* can fall off his wall and crack open, and *Jack and Jill* can climb up a hill made by laying a paper doily on the OHP screen, and roll back down again.

Photograph 10: Scene from Millie and the Spice Mice – storytelling with shadow puppets, pre-five

Shadow theatre provides an alternative storytelling method, and can be highly 'participative'. Brief stories that have a high visual content are best. Take Millie, a little mouse who is longing to go to the 'Spice Mice' disco but hasn't a thing to wear. The Fairy Mousemother tells her that she can go if she can remember in order all the objects that appear on the magic TV screen. The children have great fun trying to guess what each shadow shape will be as it gradually appears (see photograph above), then recall the shapes in turn. Or there is a wizard with a cauldron full of magic spell ingredients; a magician with a top hat from which he draws all sorts of things; or, much more down to earth, a shopping basket full of the week's groceries.

In stories for very young children I rely heavily on colour. The shadow screen is ideal for showing young children colours and reinforcing recognition, and can show them how colours mix. So the three Spice Mice at Millie's Disco each wears a dress of a different primary colour and as they dance the children can watch the 'magical' changes of colour as they overlap. A good technique for letting young children practise colour mixing themselves is achieved by making the shadow 'puppets' from black sugar paper instead of card and having the children fill cut-out spaces with cellophane or gels. For the 'Millie' story I prepare small stars with their middles cut out, and these are coloured and then stuck to the screen to decorate the disco for Millie's final 'Spice Mice' dance. Slightly older children can make larger shapes such as balloons and butterflies, if they are shown how to make folds and cut out their shapes. Children are fascinated by overlapping and thus creating a shape with three colours, even if they may not realise at the time that blue and yellow make green.

Translucent shadow puppets can be used with children as young as five, provided shapes are kept very simple. *The Lighthouse Keeper's Lunch* by Ronda Armitage is suitable for small children, who can draw enormous seagulls and colour them with felt pens, making sure the wing is drawn separately (adult supervision is essential here). In the story the lighthouse keeper's wife sends him his lunches in a basket via a long rope stretched from the house to the lighthouse, and on the way it is always raided by ravenous seagulls. The children can build up lively language sequences as the 'shadow' basket hangs on a piece of string behind the screen and two children at once 'attack' its contents with their seagulls. Thus the rich vocabulary of the book is enacted, as the seagulls 'swoop' and 'soar' and 'shriek' and 'dive'. Many picture books have an incident which will lend itself to this kind of dramatisation. Children's own imaginative drawings can also be cut out and oiled and shown on screen – provided they are big enough.

So far I have described what is in essence a 'storytelling' use of shadow theatre, much as I have described before and 'scaled down' for the needs of a very young audience. Now I want to use the rest of the chapter to describe a very different way of looking at shadow puppetry for the early years. The Reggio Emilia preschool project, based in northern Italy uses the shadow in all kinds of ways, including shadow puppetry. Internationally known for over twenty years, Reggio Emilia sees the child, in Piaget's terms, as a builder of images, each image generating other images so that children master not only 'verbal' language but countless other non-verbal languages, derived from experience. Young children are immersed in highly stimulating environments which encourage them to look at their world in a myriad of different ways.

In a reaction against 'language' experiences in the early years that can be rather sterile and prescriptive, the Reggio project seeks to give back to language the words which it needs and can use, words which 'can be silent, can fill communication, change and generate ideas'. Guido Petter of the University of Padua sums up the fascination of the shadow and the reason it plays such a large part in Reggio Emilia's system of early education:

> The fascination of *shadows* is the fascination of a world halfway between light and darkness, a zone that evades conflict and fills space with quiet discretion – a quality children like.

Great importance is given to children experiencing colour, 'till they feel it inside and out', and understanding the relationships between colours, and the effects colours have. This emphasis on images and colour is far removed from the storytelling approach. The whole notion of the shadow is explored. Observations of natural shadows out of doors can be clarified in the controlled and alterable environment of a shadow screen. According to Piaget, young children believe that shadows emanate from somewhere, eg 'the great shadow of the forest', and creep in through the window. This idea of the shadow as a 'presence' could be terrifying. To young children the shadow must seem rather like the creatures which people their dreams, which affect them and yet disappear totally on waking. To understand the shadow as an absence of light is a sophisticated concept.

Simple shapes on the screen demonstrate to children how shadows grow and shrink as they move towards and away from the light source. Coloured filters can be used to show how different colours can make a scene 'feel' different and, as discussed in Chapter 3, natural forms brought in by the children can be magnified on the OHP screen to produce quite other images. The relationship between colours is beautifully illustrated when different gels are held beside one another on the screen, showing how 'red' an orange looks when placed beside a yellow; how 'blue' a purple appears alongside a vivid red, and so on.

Young children can be helped to 'draw' with light by making holes in paper in a similar way to the 'filigree' patterns made by the older children. Small hole punches are easier than needles for little hands.

The Reggio Emilia school would argue that just as bilingualism is an asset, so each non-verbal language mastered enriches young children's verbal language. There may be silence in the darkened room but that silence need not denote a lack of communication; ideas and connections, as-yet-wordless, will be filling the darkness. An account of the Reggio Emilia approach can be found in *The Hundred Languages of Children* by Carolyn Edwards (see *Further Reading*).

Puppetry in all its forms has been described as 'getting in touch with the child within', which is why this book concludes with the Early Years. I hope I have convinced teachers and others helping children to develop and use language, of the versatility of shadow puppetry, its worth in allowing 'safe' and uninhibited communication, and the delight its magic can bring.

Shadows will never cease to be magical and mysterious to me as long as I can look at them through children's eyes. I end by listing some of the ways in which children in the Reggio Emilia project have described how they see the paradox which is the shadow:

> 'it's there and you can't hold on to it'
> 'it has a shape and it has a hundred more'
> 'it seems like it's going to obey you and then it does what it wants'
> 'it's part of the night but it's also part of the day'
> 'it's made of dark air and sky'
> 'something we carry inside ourselves and it comes out of our feet'
> 'the sun makes it be born in the morning and die at night'

What powerful magic we release when we 'let the shadows speak'!

Further reading

DFE and Welsh Office. *English in the National Curriculum*. London and Cardiff, 1995.

Edwards, Carolyn P. *The Hundred Languages of Children*. Ablex Publication Corporation, 1993

Ewart, Franzeska G. *Putli's Puppet Magic*. Glasgow, *Word Play*, 1996.

Scottish Office Education Department. *English Language 5-14*. Edinburgh, 1991.

Wizniewski, David and Donna. *Worlds of Shadow: Teaching with Shadow Puppetry*. Colorado, Teacher Ideas Press 1997.

A wide selection of puppetry books and materials can be obtained from:

Ray DaSilva, President of British UNIMA, 63 Kennedy Road, Bicester, Oxfordshire OX6 8BE

Word Play is an Expressive Arts company based in Glasgow which aims to help people of all ages use language in creative ways. It is run by the author of this book, a former Primary teacher who writes professionally for both adults and children.

Bibliography

And, Metin. Karagöz: *Turkish Shadow Theatre*. Istanbul, DOST Publications 1975.

Armitage, Ronda. *The Lighthouse Keeper's Lunch*. London, Scholastic 1977.

Blackham, Olive. *Shadow Puppets*. London, Barrie and Rockliff 1960.

Castlemilk People's History Group. *The Big Flit*. Glasgow, Workers Educational Association 1990

Department of Education, Reggio Emilia. *The Hundred Languages of Children*. Reggio Emilia, Department of Education 1987.

DFE and Welsh Office. *English in the National Curriculum*. London and Cardiff, HMSO 1995.

Erda, Bettie. *Turkish Delight: Shadow Puppets in Faces* (February). New Hampshire, Cobblestone Publishing 1989.

Ewart, Franzeska G. *Eric the Mouse's Epilepsy Adventure*. Glasgow, Word Play 1997.

Ewart, Franzeska G. *The Dragons' Colour Magic*. Glasgow, Word Play 1997.

Ewart, Franzeska G. *Millie and the Spice Mice*. Glasgow, Word Play 1997.

Klein, Gillian. *Reading into Racism*. London, Routledge 1985.

Martinovitch, Nicholas N. *The Turkish Theatre*. New York, 1933.

Reiniger, Lotte. *Shadow Theatres and Shadow Films*. London, Batsford 1970.

Reusch, Rainer. *The Rebirth of Shadows*. Schwäbisch Gmünd, UNIMA Centre 1991.

Riordan, James. *Oxford Myths and Legends: Korean Folk Tales*. London, Oxford University Press 1994

Scottish Office Education Department. *English Language 5-14*. Edinburgh, SED 1991.

Scottish Office Education Department. *A Curriculum Framework for Children in their Pre-school Year*. Edinburgh, SED 1997.

Smucker, Barbara. *Underground to Canada*. Harmondsworth, Penguin 1977.

Speaight, George. *The History of the English Puppet Theatre*. London, Robert Hale 1990.

Stoichita, Victor I. *A Short History of the Shadow*. London, Reaktion Books 1997.

Sweeney, Amin. *Malay Shadow Puppets*. London, British Museum Publications 1980.

Wizniewski, David and Donna. Worlds of Shadow: Teaching with Shadow Puppetry. Colorado, Teacher Ideas Press 1997.

INDEX

Page numbers for pictures appear in *italics*